JAPANESE PAPER YARN

Using Washi and Kami-ito to Knit, Crochet, Weave, and More

Foreword by Meher McArthur

ANDRA F. STANTON

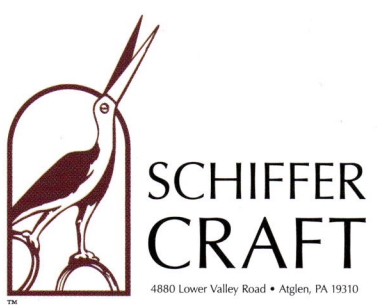

SCHIFFER
CRAFT

4880 Lower Valley Road • Atglen, PA 19310

Other Schiffer Craft Books by the Author:

Dimensional Cloth: Sculpture by Contemporary Textile Artists, foreword by Josephine Stealey,
ISBN 978-0-7643-5536-3

How Art Heals: Exploring Your Deep Feelings Using Collage, foreword by Tien Chiu,
ISBN 978-0-7643-6146-3

Other Schiffer Craft Books on Related Subjects:

Weaving Paper: 13 Upcycled Projects with Scrap Paper, Dorothea Katharina Schmidt,
ISBN 978-0-7643-6804-2

The Art of Kintsugi: Learning the Japanese Craft of Beautiful Repair, Alexandra Kitty,
ISBN 978-0-7643-6054-1

Painting with Paper: Paper on the Edge, Yulia Brodskaya, ISBN 978-0-7643-5854-8

Designed by Llara Pazdan
Cover design by Ashley Millhouse & Molly Shields
Type set in Bourton Hand/Meta Serif Pro

Front cover photo: Nate Castner.
Back cover photos: Nate Castner. *Top left:* Crocheted Square Basket by Ulrike Hagel; *top right*: Pulped Paper Weaving by Jennifer Davies. *Bottom left*: Knitted Cable Twine Scarf by Cat Ohala; *bottom right*: Knitted Vase Cover by Barbara Olson.

ISBN: 978-0-7643-6830-1
978-1-5073-0400-6 ePub

Printed in India

MIX
Paper | Supporting responsible forestry
FSC™ C016779
www.fsc.org

Published by Schiffer Craft
An imprint of Schiffer Publishing, Ltd.
4880 Lower Valley Road
Atglen, PA 19310
Phone: (610) 593-1777; Fax: (610) 593-2002
Email: Info@schifferbooks.com
Web: www.schifferbooks.com

For our complete selection of fine books on this and related subjects, please visit our website at www.schifferbooks.com. You may also write for a free catalog.

Schiffer Publishing's titles are available at special discounts for bulk purchases for sales promotions or premiums. Special editions, including personalized covers, corporate imprints, and excerpts, can be created in large quantities for special needs. For more information, contact the publisher.

We are always looking for people to write books on new and related subjects. If you have an idea for a book, please contact us at proposals@schifferbooks.com.

To all who are curious,
brave, and compassionate

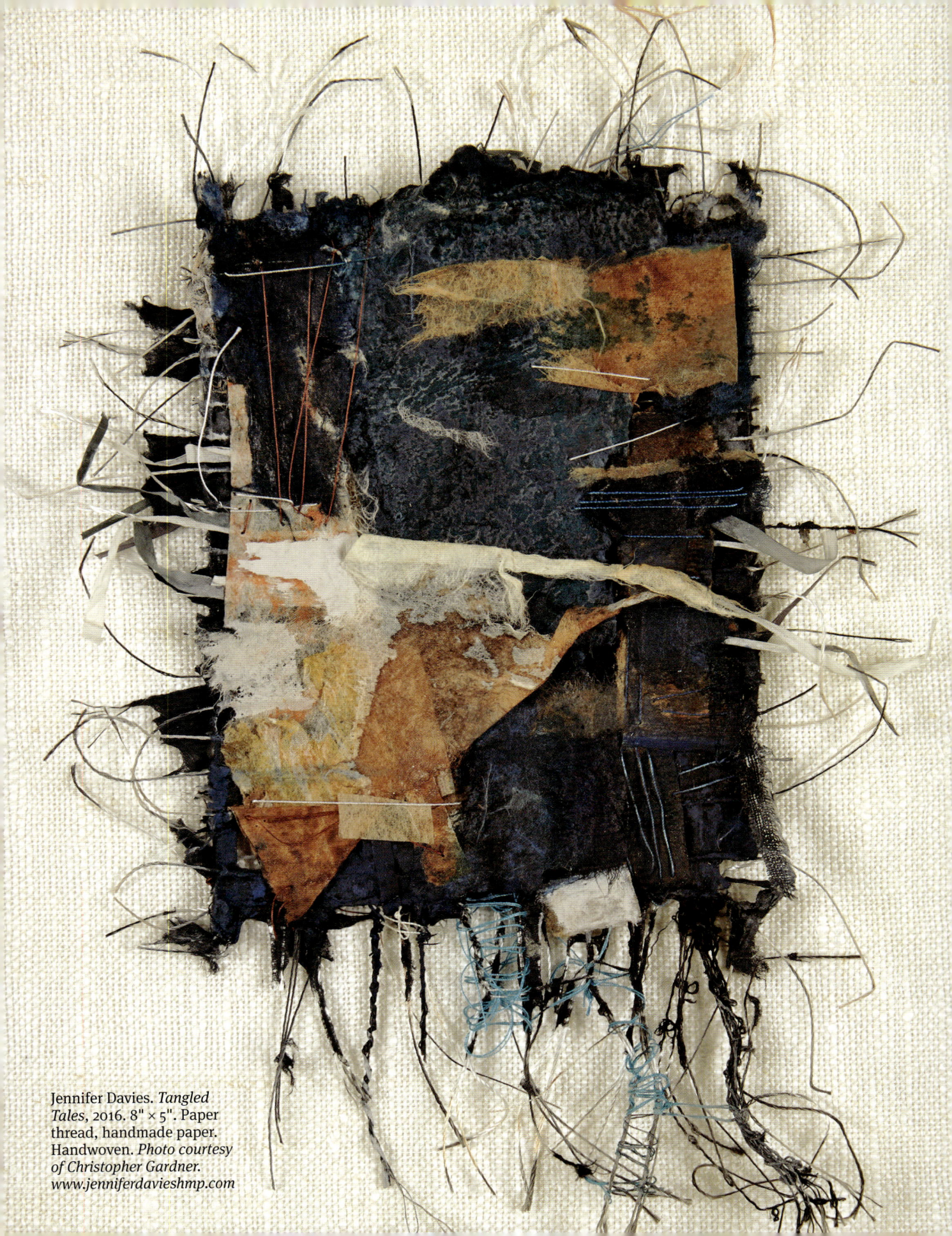

Jennifer Davies. *Tangled Tales*, 2016. 8" × 5". Paper thread, handmade paper. Handwoven. *Photo courtesy of Christopher Gardner.* www.jenniferdavieshmp.com

CONTENTS

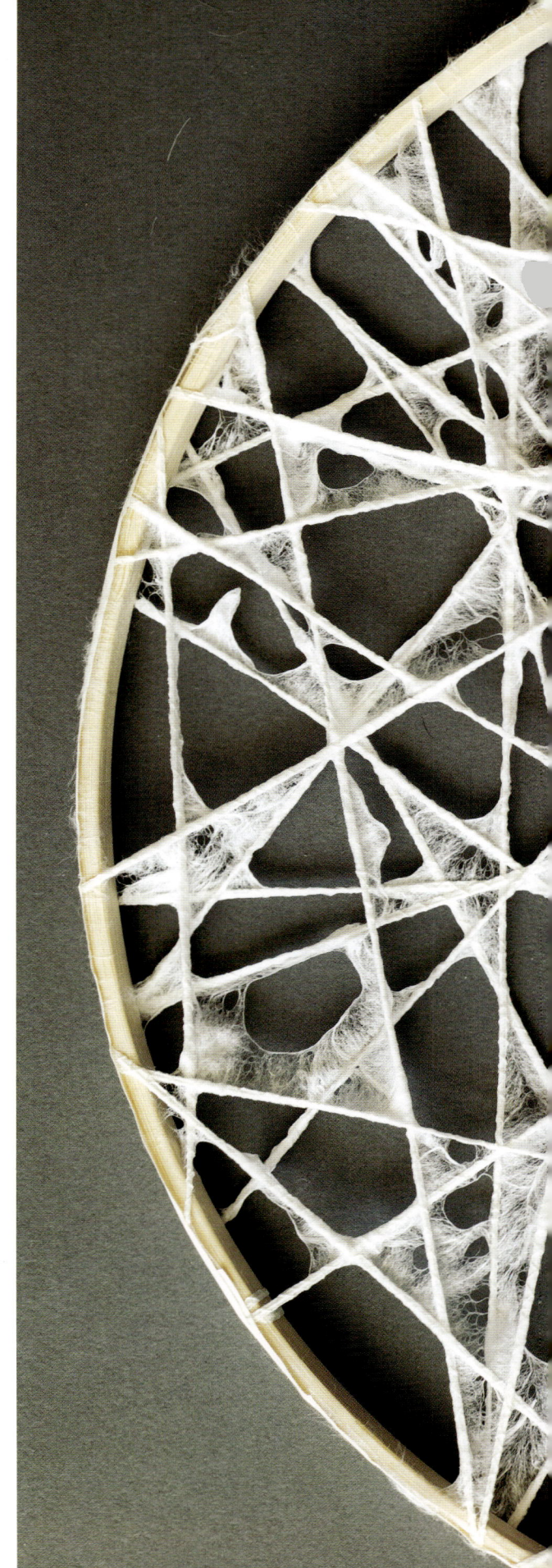

FOREWORD

Shifu, or paper cloth, is one of Japan's less familiar artforms. Little is known about its history because of the fragile nature of paper and the relatively low financial value of the cloth; however, this tradition—in which a natural fiber is transformed into paper, reworked into a human-made fiber, and then woven into cloth—is a fascinating chapter in the history of Japanese fiber art.

In Asia, paper is usually made from plant fibers that are softened into a pulp and felted together on a mat or screen. Because the fibers are not broken down, but retain their length and become interwoven with each other during the papermaking process, traditional Asian papers tend to be strong and textured. In China, where paper was invented in 8 BCE, the earliest fibers used were hemp, paper mulberry (*Broussonetia papyrifera*), and rattan. Later, bamboo and paper mulberry were predominant sources.

Paper was introduced to Japan as early as the third and fourth centuries, and papermaking techniques, sometime between the fifth and eighth centuries. Since then, Japanese paper has been made primarily of paper mulberry fibers, or *kozo*, although *gampi* (*Diplomorpha sikokiana*) and *mitsumata* (*Edgeworthia chrysantha*) have also been significant in papermaking over the centuries.

In traditional Japanese papermaking, the bark is first steamed and the darker outer sections removed. The remaining fibers are rinsed, cooked until soft, and then beaten to break the fibers into pulp made up of thin strands. The fiber pulp is mixed into a vat of water to create a water suspension. A bamboo sieve-like screen is dunked into the suspension and drawn up, catching some of the pulp on the surface of the screen, while the water drains away.

Around the eighth century, Japanese papermakers invented the *nagashizuki*, or discharge, technique in which they added a vegetable substance called *neri* to the suspension and then maneuvered the screen skillfully to keep the fiber mixture in constant motion, resulting in sheets of paper that are thin, translucent, and very strong. Each sheet was removed from the screen and left to dry and bleach in the sun. Paper sheets have been used customarily in Japan not only as a surface for writing text and drawing images, but also in architecture, clothing, lighting, toys, and many other areas of daily life. In the late nineteenth century, to distinguish Japanese handmade paper from Western paper, it became known as *washi* (和紙)—meaning, Japanese paper.

Closely related to the creation of *washi* is the practice of paper thread making, or *kami-ito* (紙糸). Hair ties made of paper threads were mentioned in poetry anthologies dating from the eighth to the tenth century and were likely used by ladies of the imperial court. Around the same time, courtiers also began using twisted paper cords, called *mizuhiki*, in gift-giving and ceremonial rituals. Made of different colors—usually red, white, black, and gold—these cords were crafted from paper, stiffened with glue, and wrapped around gifts and offerings.

Because threads were made of paper at this early date, it is very likely that *shifu* (紙布) was also created at this time. A sheet of paper was cut—zigzagging back and forth across the sheet to create a single, long strip—which was then spun into paper thread. To make paper cloth, these paper threads were woven, either as the warp (vertical threads in the weave) or the weft (horizontal threads in the weave) or as both. Often, paper threads were combined with other fibers such as hemp (*asa-jifu*) or cotton (*men-jifu*) and, rarely, silk (*kinu-jifu*). *Shifu* woven with both paper warp and weft is called *moro-jifu*.

Members of Japan's imperial court had access to soft, luxurious silk fabric for their lavish robes. It is unlikely that they wore *shifu* garments. Most of the surviving examples of *shifu* are garments of the type worn by farmers, fishermen, and other laborers. By weaving in paper threads, they added warmth and durability to their garments. These jackets (*haori*, and the thicker *hanten*) and sashes (*obi*) were often dyed indigo blue, and in many cases combined paper threads with hemp and cotton threads.

However, in the district of Shiroishi, near Sendai in northern Japan, where very high-quality paper has been made since the seventeenth century, a tradition of *shifu* woven by samurai families from threads made from local paper also thrived at that time. These fine *shifu* garments were worn by members of the samurai class and, occasionally, were presented as gifts to the imperial court and the military government. The practice of constructing high-quality *shifu* garments has continued in Shiroishi and in a handful of other regions until the present day, and—despite the humble origins of the materials—these garments have been luxury items.

In the early decades of the twentieth century, Western clothing began to replace traditional Japanese dress, and machine-made Western paper largely supplanted labor-intensive and expensive *washi*. Today, only a few families in scattered regions of Japan produce customary handmade paper, and very few artisans create paper threads or weave *shifu* cloth. However, concern by local and national government agencies to preserve traditional arts and crafts, as well as a

growing interest and support from foreign visitors, overseas collectors, and arts-and-crafts makers are bolstering these traditions and encouraging younger generations to continue working in this time-honored industry.

—Meher McArthur

Independent Japanese art curator, author, and educator
Los Angeles, California

ACKNOWLEDGMENTS

A heartfelt thank you to my generous, enthusiastic contributing professional and nonprofessional artists.

A huge thank you, too, to Nate Castner, Helen Heibert, David Hoffend, Kakuko Ishii, Nancy Jacobi, Donna Koretsky, Meher McArthur, Karen Trask, Linda Thalmann, Tran Hong Nhung, Cat Ohala, Jill Powers, and Zoe Ann Stiver; and Fiber Fusion Northwest, Hiromi Paper, the Textile Society of America, and Washi Arts.

Once again, thank you to Sandra Korinchak at Schiffer Books for her sensitivity, encouragement, and support. And to Schiffer's design team—the best book design team ever.

Last, a great big thanks to my friends Becca Alexander, Carol Eaton, Jody Berman, Andrea and Dana Meyers, Phyllis Goldfarb, Bridget Gordon, Sandra Petrucelli, Sally Nelson, Joellen Roundtree, and Margareta Bancroft. Thank you for your love, kindness, enthusiasm, and support. It means the world to me.

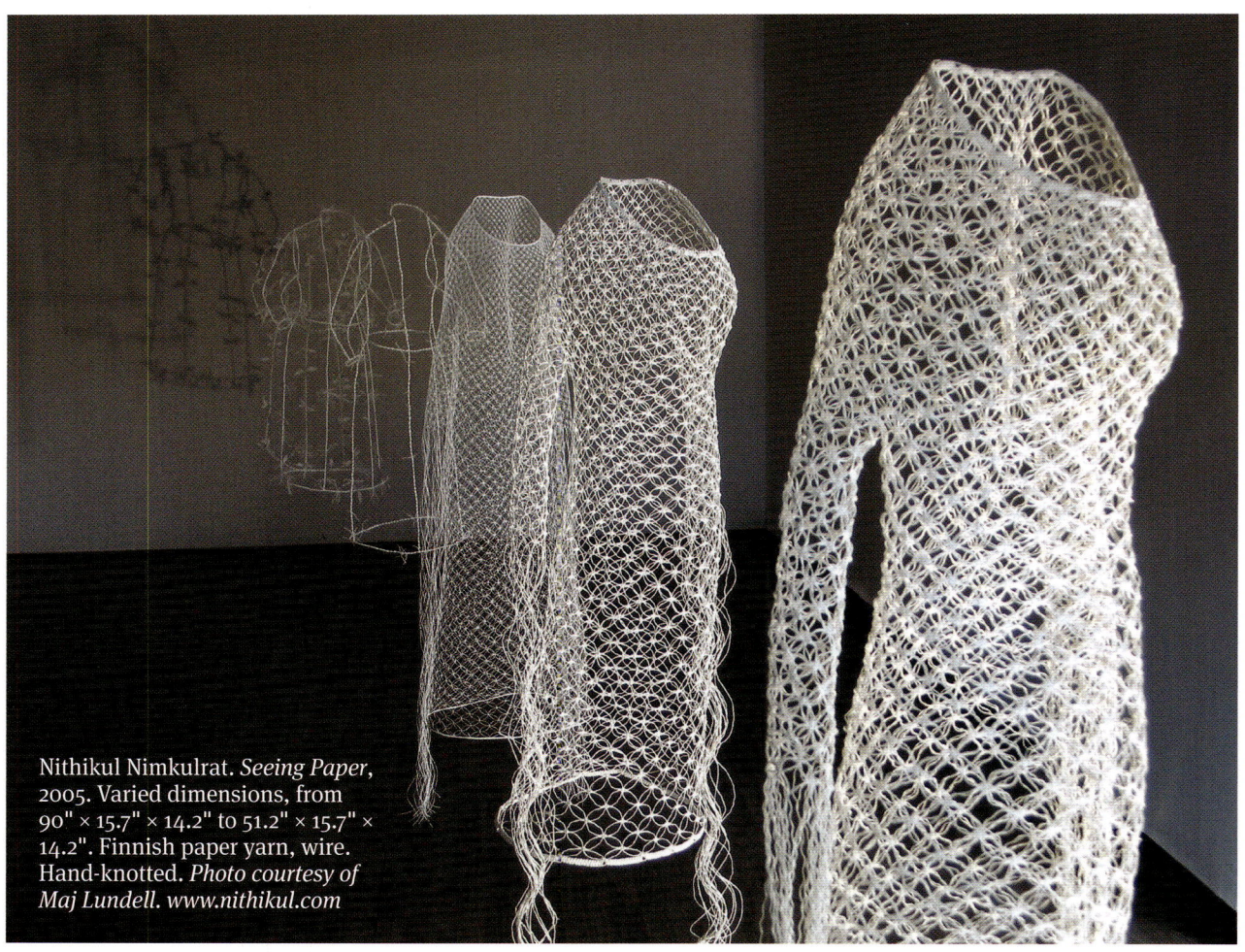

Nithikul Nimkulrat. *Seeing Paper*, 2005. Varied dimensions, from 90" × 15.7" × 14.2" to 51.2" × 15.7" × 14.2". Finnish paper yarn, wire. Hand-knotted. *Photo courtesy of Maj Lundell. www.nithikul.com*

ABOUT THIS BOOK

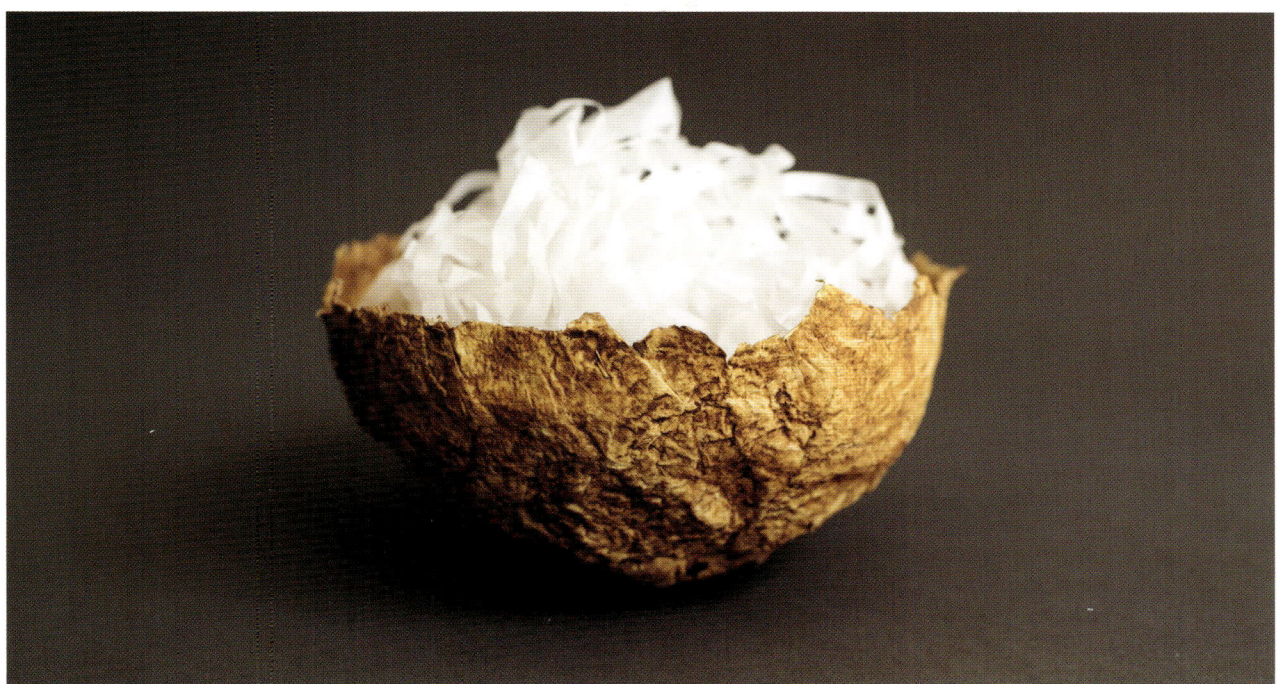

Welcome to the world of Japanese paper yarn. It is my pleasure to share with you information about the use of paper yarn in Japanese contemporary art as well as some history behind this remarkable artform.

I think of myself as a champion of artists creating interesting, unusual, and beautiful art. Scientific research tells us that art heals by increasing pleasure hormones (dopamine) and by decreasing stress hormones (cortisol), but those of us who are artists already know this intuitively. Making and viewing art fills us with wonder and joy, taps into our sadness and pain, and gives a visual voice to our deepest feelings. With the support and kindness of others who share and value art, we can reap the pleasure of affinity and connection.

My purpose in writing this book is to show my appreciation of and respect for the history of papermaking in Asia. It is not, and never will be, an attempt to appropriate a culture's heritage. My intent is to bring to light—to a new audience—the history of and creations produced using paper yarn, and to showcase some of the artists who work with it.

Contained within are an overview of the history of making paper, twelve how-to projects with instructions, and photos of creations by artists to inspire you. The how-to projects are rated by skill level: **beginner** (easy enough for any craftsperson to replicate), **intermediate** (requires some knowledge of a craft skill, such as weaving, knitting, or crocheting), and **experienced** (requires extensive knowledge of particular craft skills).

I promise you will love the challenge of exploring and innovating with paper yarn.

INTRODUCTION

A few years ago, I came home from visiting a friend and artist, and announced excitedly to my husband that we had made paper.

"That's amazing!" he said. "What did you make it out of?"

My answer: "Paper."

"Oh," he said, as he rolled his eyes. "That's . . . great."

But it *was* great. I guess I'd missed the opportunity as a kid. I didn't have any cool teachers who showed me how to pulp paper, disperse the goop onto a screen, drain off the water, and turn it out to dry. But now, as an adult, I was gobsmacked by both the process and the result: a highly textured sheet with lovely, uneven edges and, with more experimentation, gorgeous inclusions such as dried rose petals, pressed flowers, or grass seeds.

Since then, I've been making paper, not just *from* paper, but from nearly anything I can find in my backyard, including milkweed (*Asclepias syriaca*) stalks, Hosta leaves and stems, and ornamental grasses (*Pennisetum setaceum and Cortaderia selloana)*. I also buy abaca pulp (a natural-color fiber, also known as *manilla hemp*, derived from banana plant leaf stalks) and cotton linter (an organic fiber derived from cotton). And I cannot pass up a pile of mail! All those envelopes, bills, and statements make wonderful pulp.

Playing with these materials has given me a great appreciation of what the earliest papermakers must have gone through during their own investigations of the varied fibers from which they tried to fashion paper. And not just the materials, but also the processes to separate the bark from inner fibers, to clean and soften the fibers, and to form them into sheets with additions that keep them suspended in water, helping with uniform alignment and consequent paper strength. There is *so* much to consider!

Furthermore, my interest in papermaking engendered curiosity about handmade paper cordage: yarn, string, twine, thread, and the like. The word *thread* goes back centuries and stems from the concept of *twisting*. By twisting bits together, you get not only a longer bit, but also a stronger one. The utility of such cording is immense. Nearly anything can be made from it—from clothing and linens to high-speed internet cables.

"Everybody knows about fire and the wheel, but string is one of the most powerful tools and really the most overlooked," said Saskia Wolsak, an ethnobiologist. "It's relatively invisible until you start looking for it. Then you see it everywhere."[1]

Like paper, thread has been and can be made from a huge variety of plant materials. Also like paper, the process of making it requires a great deal of time, work, and experience.

I've made thread from mulberry papers, but I've seen thread made from iris leaves; bindweed, nettle, and dandelion stems; milkweed fluff; coffee filters; teabag paper; corn husks; daylily leaves; seaweed; cattail leaves; young grape vines; flax; young honeysuckle vines; hemp stems; preflowering blackberry stems; and dogbane.

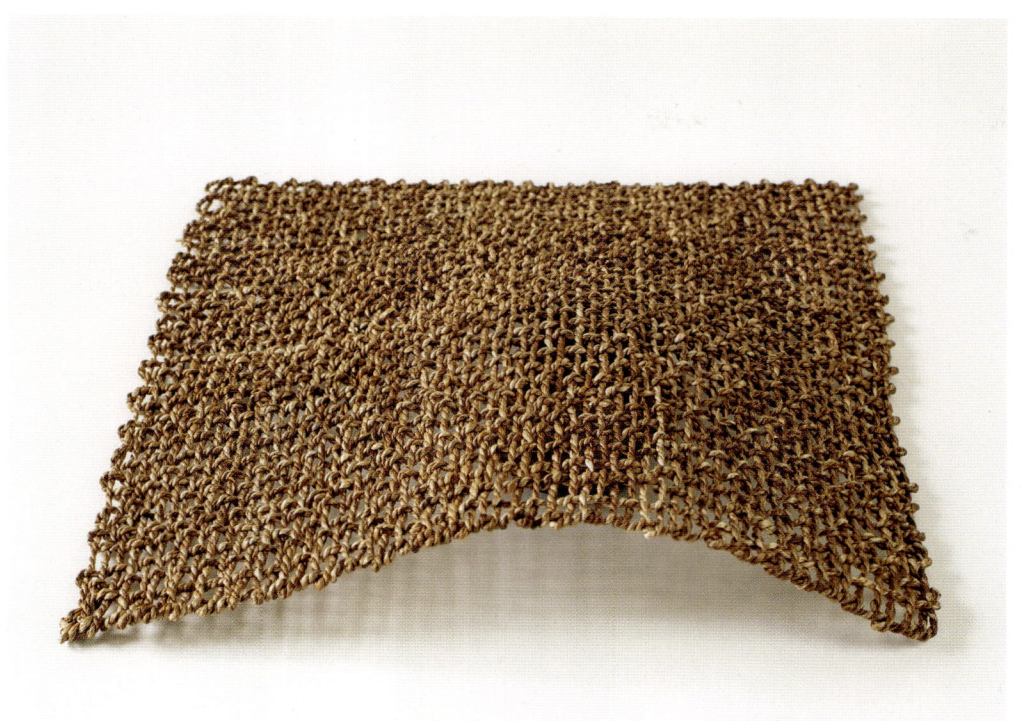

Alice Fox. *Dandelion Weave 3*, 2021. 11.8" × 11.8". Cordage from hand-twisted dandelion stems (*Taraxacum officinale*) woven in one continuous warp–weft structure. *Photo courtesy of Sarah Mason. www.alicefox .co.uk*

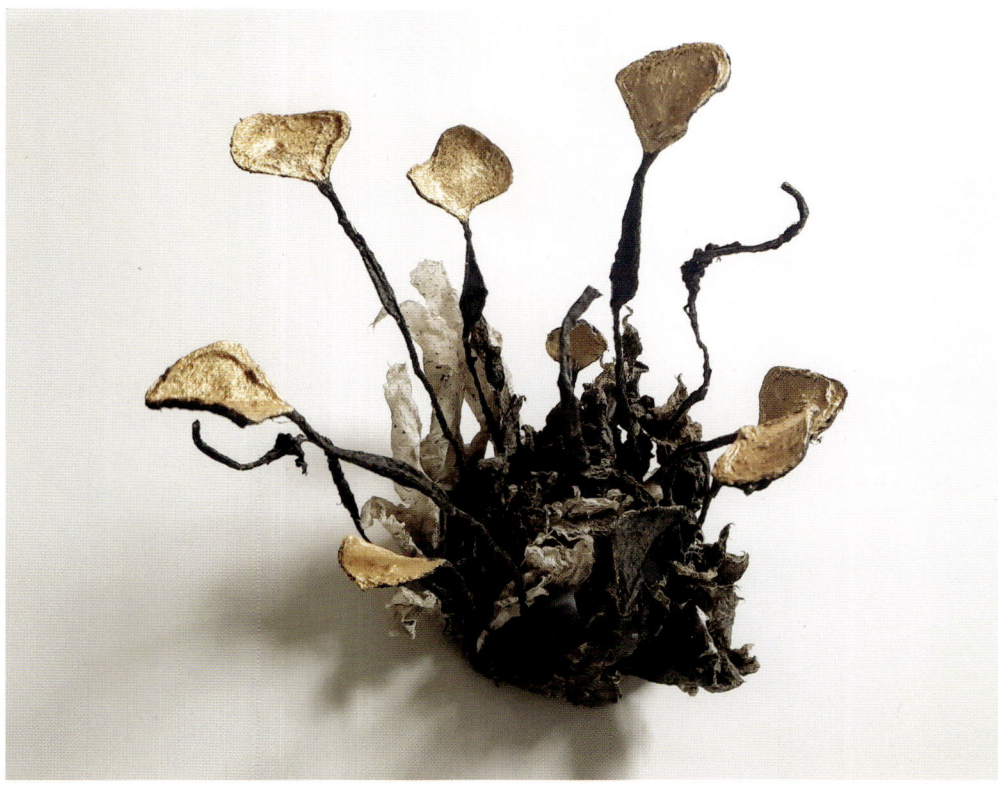

May Babcock. *Water Chestnut Studies*, 2021. 38" × 38" × 8". Artist-made paper from pondweed fiber, wire. *Photo courtesy of May Babcock. www.maybabcock.com*

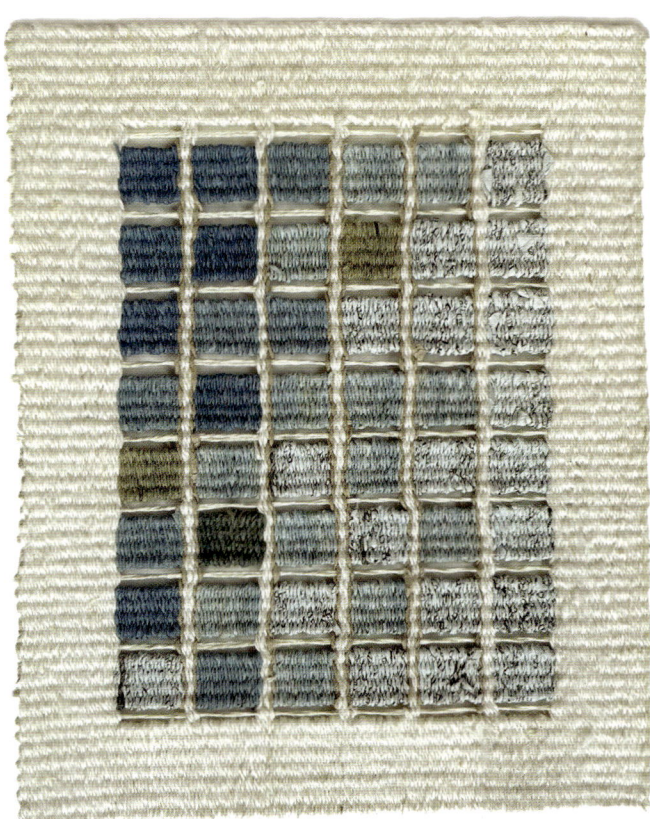

Sarah C. Swett. *Paper Blues*, 2020. 6" × 5". Hand-spun using coffee filters, variable annuity quarterly report pages, indigo, natural pigments, linen warp. Handwoven tapestry. *Photograph courtesy of Sarah C. Swett. www.afieldguidetoneedlework.com*

I wasn't always interested in paper and paper thread—that is, until I attended a museum show traveling across the country called *Washi Transformed: New Expressions in Japanese Paper*. It was a celebration of paper and the artists who have been exploring it.

As McArthur and Goodall note in their catalog for the show, up until recently, the role of Japanese paper in art has been secondary to the image or text applied to its surface using ink. The paper itself has rarely been considered a significant factor in evaluating the piece's artistic value.[2]

However, *Washi Transformed* proved times have changed. The artists included in the show see *washi* not merely as a surface on which to write, draw, or paint, but as a primary focus of their work. They transform this paper into sculptures, installations, and highly textured wall hangings that demonstrate the endless possibilities of this medium in contemporary art.

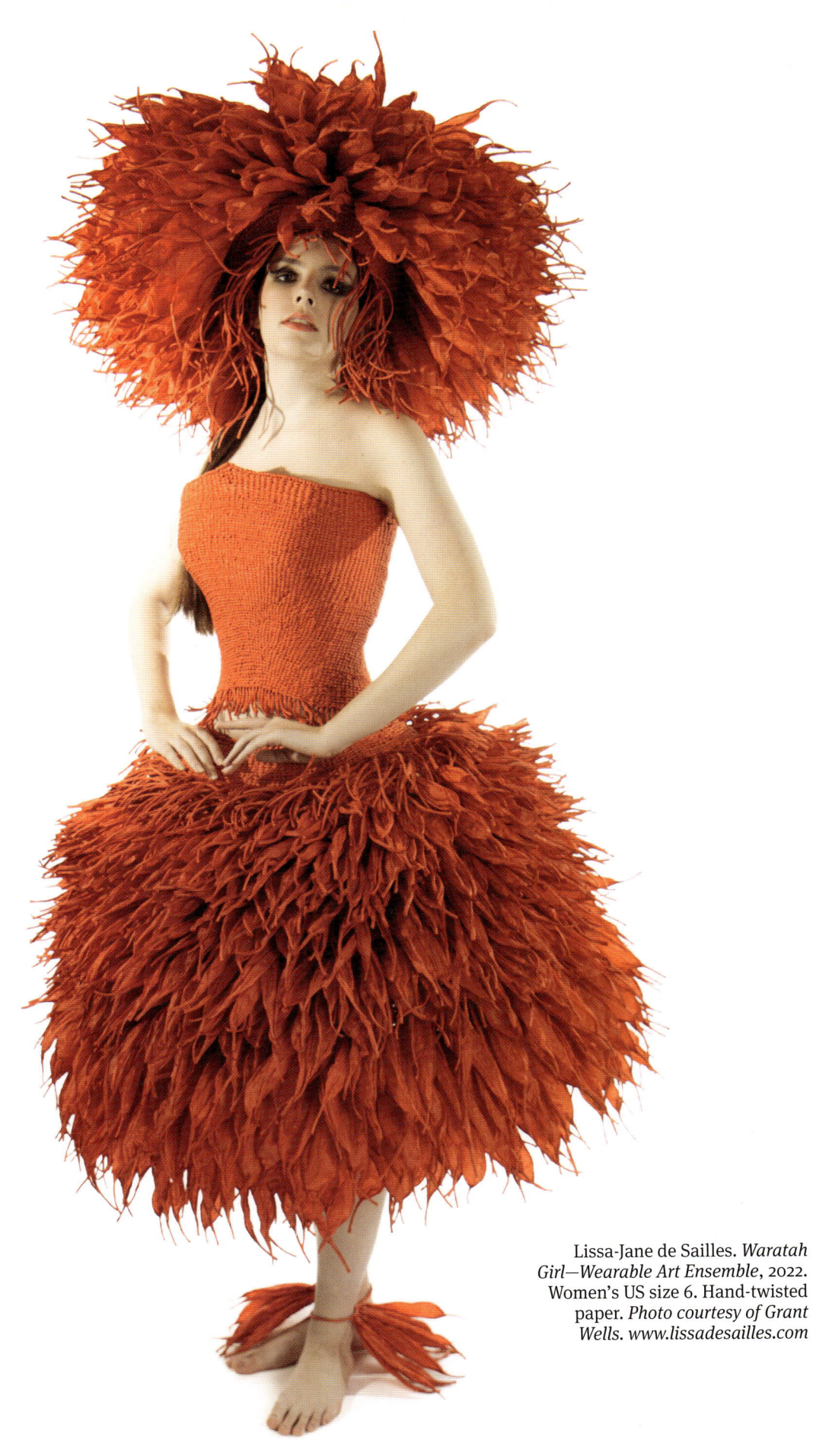

Lissa-Jane de Sailles. *Waratah Girl—Wearable Art Ensemble*, 2022. Women's US size 6. Hand-twisted paper. *Photo courtesy of Grant Wells. www.lissadesailles.com*

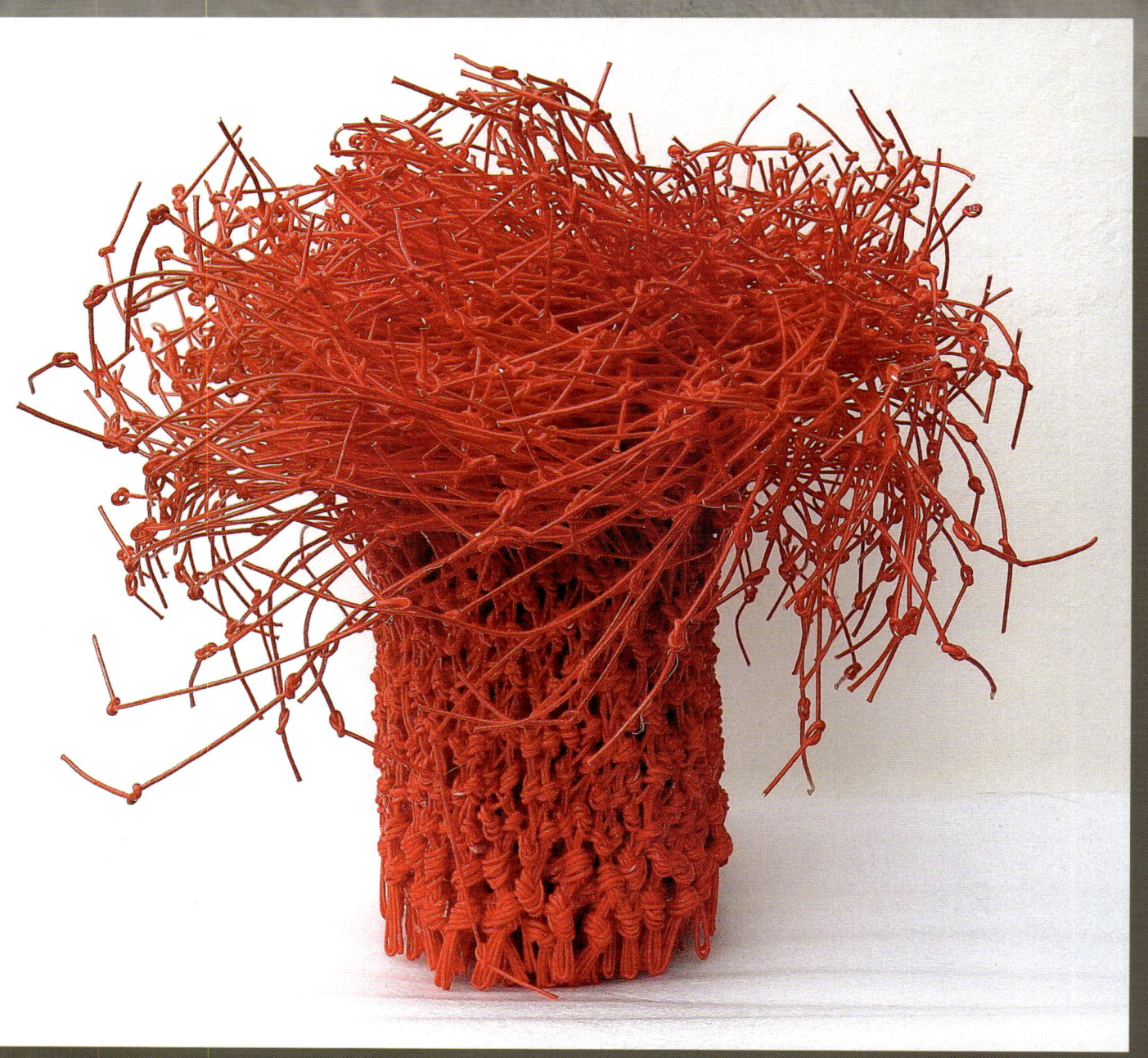

Kakuko Ishii. *Musubu R*, 2012. 7.9" × 7.9" × 7.9". Washi (mizuhiki) and pigment. *Photo courtesy of Kakuko Ishii.*

CHAPTER 1

Mizuhiki

Among my favorite pieces at the *Washi Transformed* exhibition were the knotted, lacquered sculptures created by Kakuko Ishii, an artist whose paper works have been shown in fiber art exhibitions around the world since 1978. She made her sculptures of twisted, stiffened paper cords called *mizuhiki*, which were invented in the eighth or ninth century in the Japanese imperial court—a period characterized by the flourishing culture of the court aristocracy that engaged actively in the pursuit of aesthetic refinement, leading to new developments in art and literature.

However, Ishii's *mizuhiki* are not typical of the craft. With their clean lines and multiple knots, her gathered lacquered cords become freestanding sculptures that would fit comfortably in a minimalistic contemporary setting. Yet, they also bring to mind the warm, natural shape of wheat bundles associated with more humble, rustic environs.

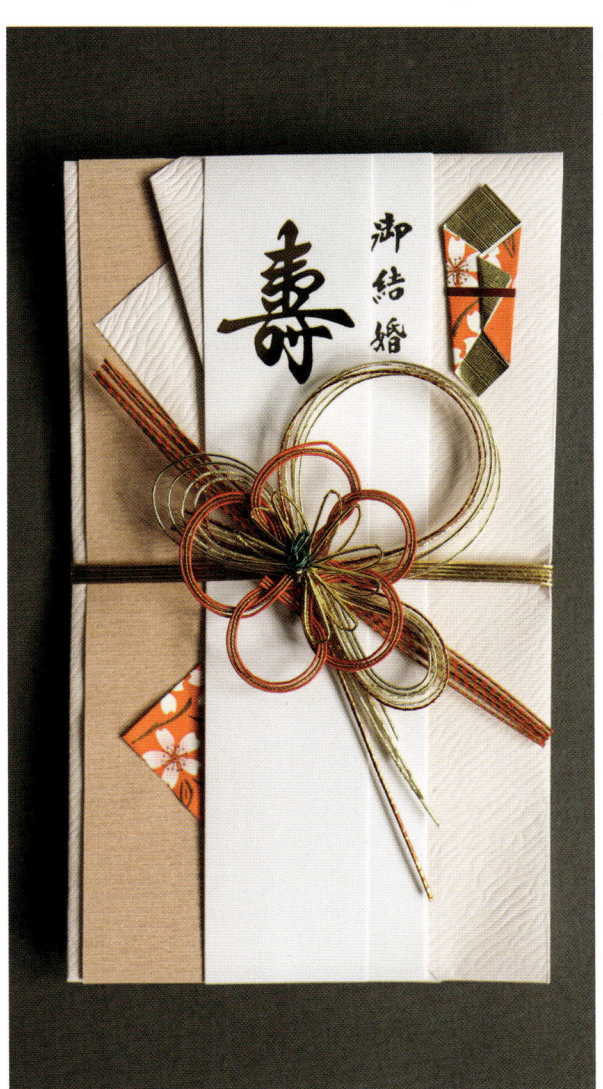

Mizuhiki, 4.5" × 8", with noshi (top right corner) and envelope for a monetary wedding gift. *Photo courtesy of Nate Castner.*

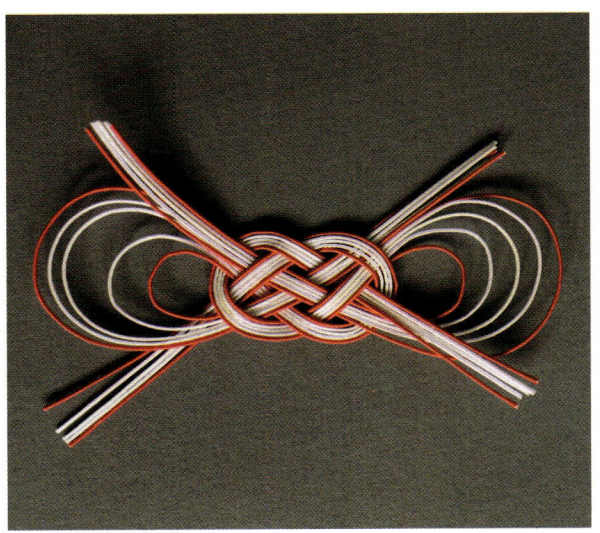

Satoi Adams (Kobayashi). *Awaiji Musubi*, 2003. 5" × 2.5". A traditional mizuhiki knot. *Photo courtesy of Nate Castner. www.mizuhikigloballinks.com*

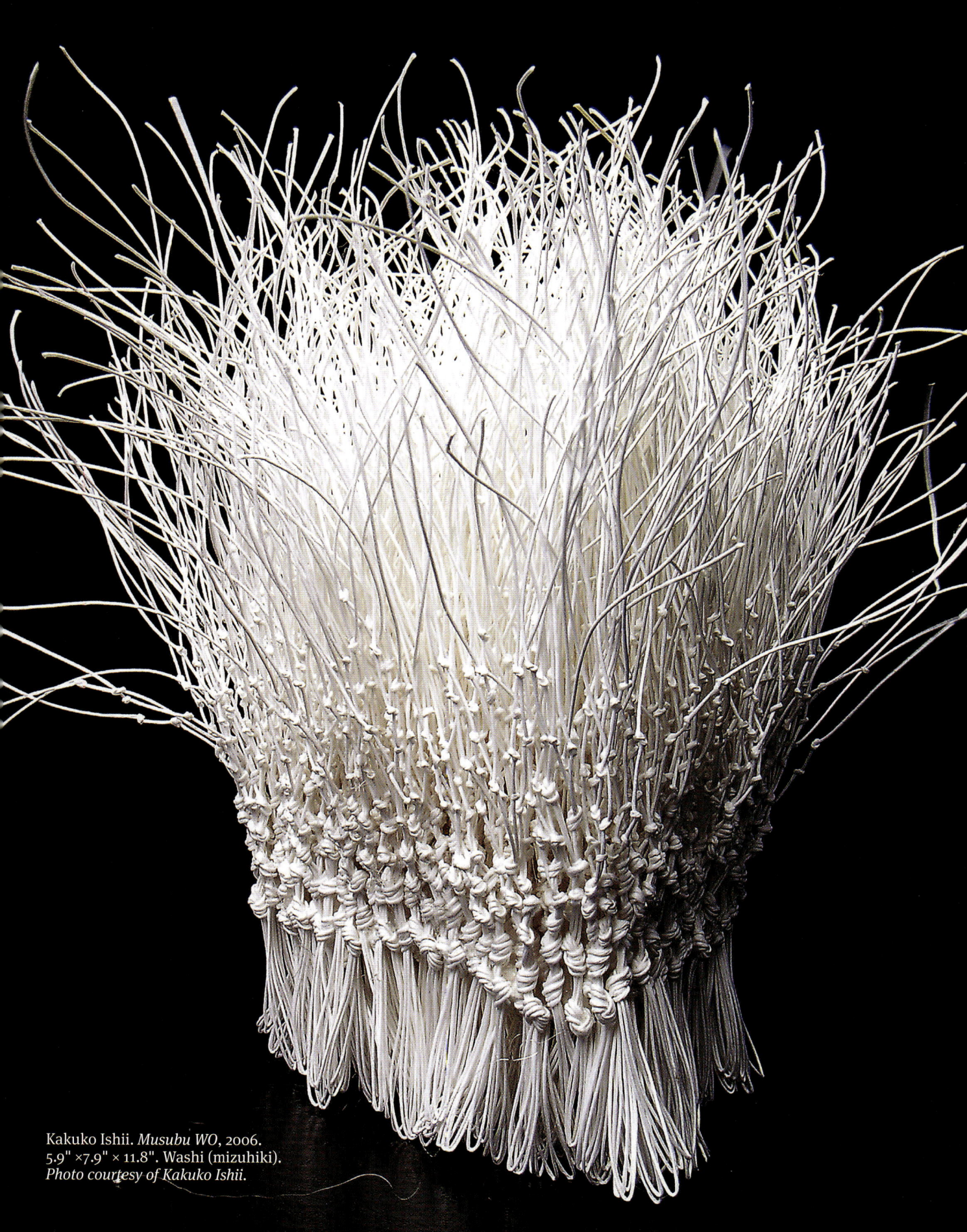

Kakuko Ishii. *Musubu WO*, 2006.
5.9" ×7.9" × 11.8". Washi (mizuhiki).
Photo courtesy of Kakuko Ishii.

Typical *mizuhiki* are created using mass-produced machine-made paper. Twisted, narrow lengths of paper are strengthened and stiffened with a fine white clay mixed with glue. When dry, they are coated with colored mylar, paint, or lacquer. Traditional colors included red, white, black, and gold. The rainbow of colors used today was introduced at the end of the Second World War.

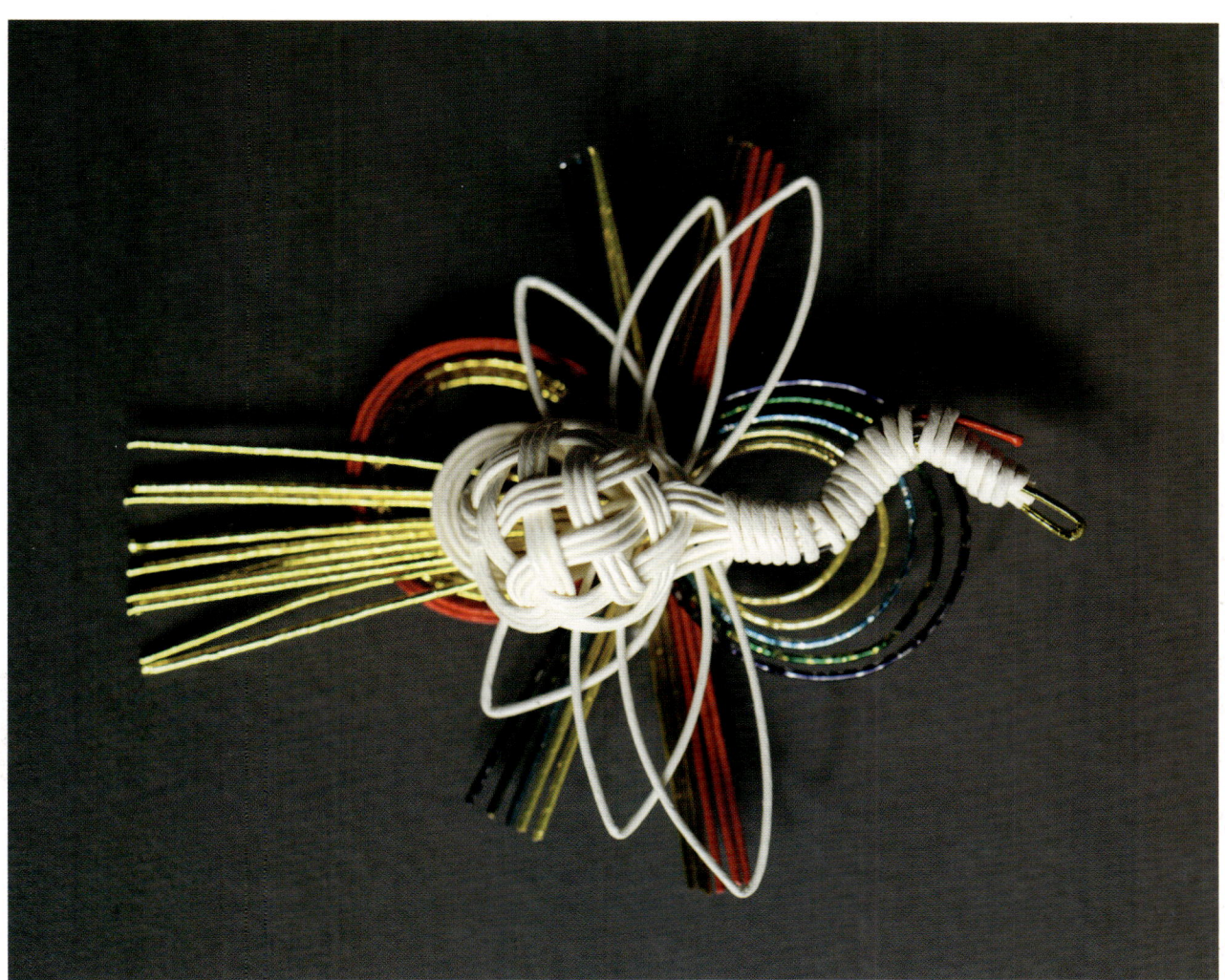

Lorraine Fukuwa. *Mizuhiki Crane*, 4" × 3.3". *Photo courtesy of Nate Castner. www.ebay.com (Lolosteve)*

CHAPTER 2

Japanese Paper

A world without paper is unimaginable. Whether it's in the form of books, newspapers, journals, or magazines; gift wrapping; sketching, watercolor, and mixed-media art paper; business and greeting cards; paper plates and cups; freezer and parchment paper; napkins, paper towels, and so on, we rely on paper in its many forms.

Despite the huge potential for a global reduction in the use of paper with the availability of digital media, whether by replacing a catalog with an online shop, advertising on the internet rather than in magazines or direct mail, or delivering all kinds of information in electronic form, it is estimated that digital applications currently replace only twenty-five percent of paper consumption.[3]

Why not more? Besides the fact that paper represents knowledge and culture, we love how it looks and feels. It has texture, a vividness (or not) of color and finish, and a comforting turn-the-page factor that websites and emails can't come close to reproducing. In short, many people like paper better.

For a countless number of us, the smell of a paper book is enchanting. The aroma is so popular that perfumiers have tried to capture the essence of a book's smell through scented candles and even cologne. In fact, a study at Temple University using functional magnetic resonance images to determine the differences in the impact that digital and print media have on the human brain showed that paper was found to activate the part of the brain most associated with desire.[4]

Yet, as much as Americans love paper, Japanese love it even more. In fact, Japanese culture has been said to be built on wood and paper, alluding to the fact that forests cover close to seventy percent of Japan's land area, contributing to its unique architecture and sundry wood-based products, including sushi rice barrels and bathtubs, as well as the pervasiveness of paper in everyday life.

Some 700 years before the Gutenberg Bible was printed in 1455, the Japanese were hand-printing Buddhist texts on paper. Before printed periodicals began to appear in Europe in the seventeenth century as predecessors of the modern newspaper, Japan was printing *yomiuri*, or dailies, sold in major urban centers. Today, Japan maintains the largest circulation of print newspapers in the world, and boasts the second largest circulation per capita. Paper has a long history all over the world, but, to Japan, it is what wine is to the French—a national obsession and point of pride.

After the process of making paper was created and refined, it ultimately became a part of nearly every aspect of Japanese life. For example, folded paper, or origami, was used by warriors during the Kamakura period (1185–1333) to wrap their shields. Papers folded in zigzag shapes were hung vertically in the entranceway of Shinto shrines during the Muromachi period (1333–1573). During the Edo period (1603–1868), origami became a hobby for the masses.

Centuries ago, because Japan had no sheep for wool, cotton did not grow well, and silk was reserved for the upper classes, clothing was often made from paper as well. Such paper yarn, called *kami-ito*, was treated with *konyaku*, a gelatin-like substance from the root vegetable *konjac* (pronounced *konyack*), which made it strong and

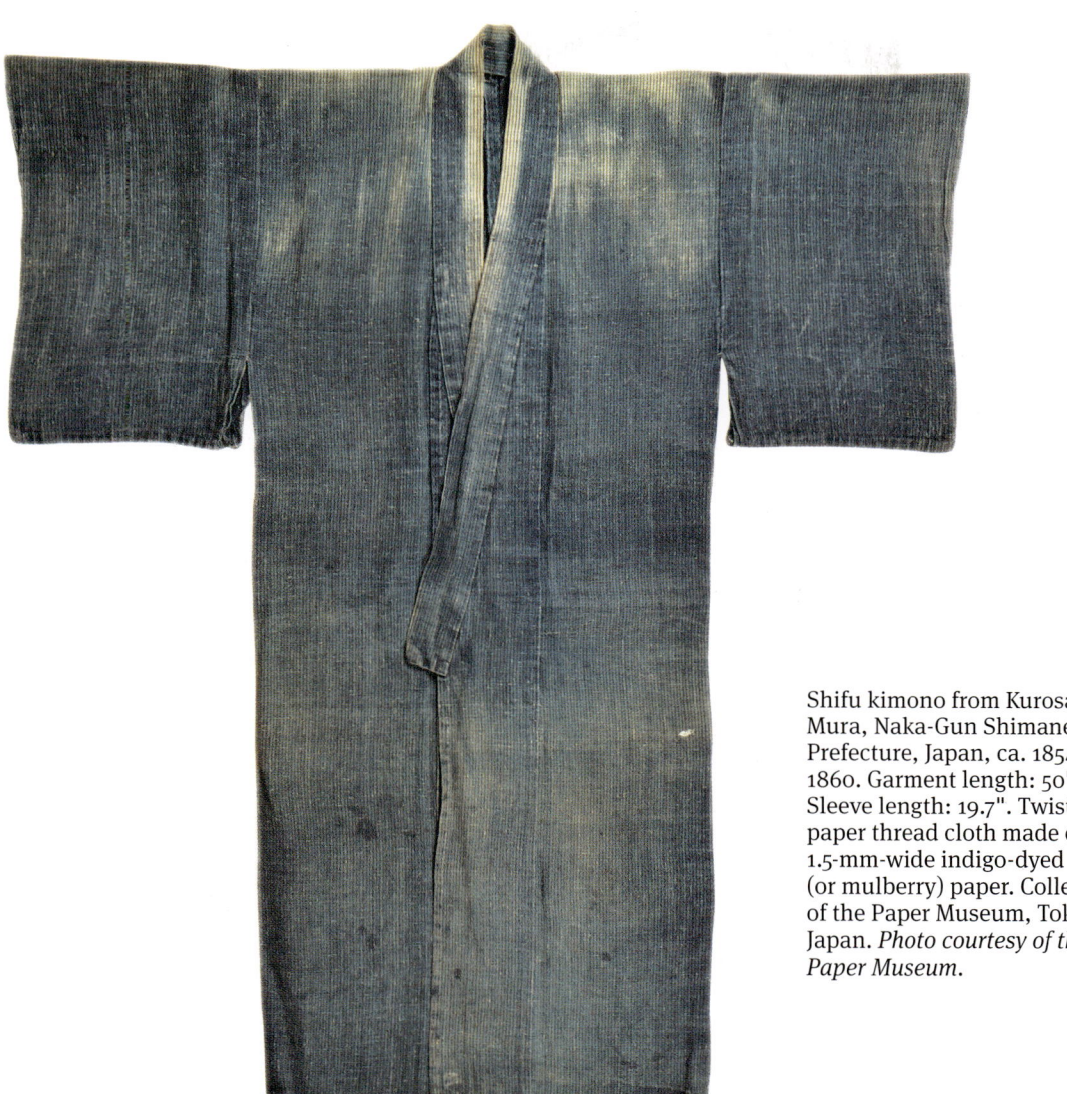

Shifu kimono from Kurosawa-Mura, Naka-Gun Shimane Prefecture, Japan, ca. 1854–1860. Garment length: 50". Sleeve length: 19.7". Twisted paper thread cloth made of 1.5-mm-wide indigo-dyed *kozo* (or mulberry) paper. Collection of the Paper Museum, Tokyo, Japan. *Photo courtesy of the Paper Museum.*

waterproof. The resulting woven fabric was breathable, yet protected the wearer from rain, wind, and cold temperatures.

Paper also became a widely used building material. *Shoji* screens, which were ubiquitous during the Edo period, contributed to the clean lines that later attracted Modernist architects such as Le Corbusier to traditional Japanese architecture. Paper carpets were used as a substitute for cloth. Paper replaced leather for bags, such as tobacco pouches, and was later modified and developed into wallpaper during the Meiji period (1868–1912).

Kaminagato, a paper substitute for wood and metal, was used to make weapons. It was created by layering paper onto a bamboo or wooden support that was then covered in lacquer. This method was also used to make boxes, plates, bowls, tea containers, helmets worn as fire protection, canteens, sake containers and cups, lunch boxes, desks, and hats.

The list goes on and on. In the introduction to his book *A Papermaking Pilgrimage to Japan, Korea and China* Dard Hunter wrote, "It is not an exaggeration to state that the present-day handmade papers of Japan are the technical marvel of the entire papermaker's craft."[5]

In Japanese culture, paper has always been associated with spirituality. *Kami* is the Japanese word for an actual piece of paper, but it also translates to "divinity." In ancient Japan, it was linked to Shintoism, the country's original religion. Shintoism's foundational idea was that all things, including people, animals, plants, and objects, are inhabited by gods (*kami*). Shintoism was eventually replaced by Buddhism, around 538 CE, when paper became honored as the mediator between God and people.

In 1969, *washi* calligraphy paper was designated a National Important Intangible Cultural Asset by UNESCO. In 2014, in accordance with a UNESCO treaty, it was deemed an Intangible Heritage of Humanity. Such a designation indicates the object, word(s), or process is considered an important cultural treasure and an essential component of creative diversity and expression.[6] Other recipients of this designation include sericulture, the traditional production of silk for weaving; couscous (small, rolled granules of wheat flour used in Maghrebi cuisine); and Argentina's tango.

In the late 1800s, there were more than 100,000 families making paper by hand. But, with the introduction from Europe of mechanized papermaking technology, production declined. Up until the early 1900s, *washi* was made by only a few hundred Japanese families. By the early 2000s, this number was holding steady at around 350. These families struggle to compete in the world market with handmade papers from India, Thailand, and Nepal, where a lower cost of living makes it possible to produce paper more cheaply.

Young papermakers, however, are now entering the field, many of whom are not from papermaking families, as has been the tradition. A good many of the creators come to papermaking after studying other subjects in universities, such as interior design, graphic design, engineering, printmaking, and science. Others are attracted to this profession as an alternative to what they consider "a numbing urban life devoid of meaning and purpose, and far away from nature, beauty, and working with one's hands."[7]

Although this burgeoning interest in revitalizing the field is exciting, it is also true that it is accompanied by a decline in the number of users of handmade paper because of its expense, as well as a decrease in the quality of the paper. Some senior papermakers see the younger generations as competitors and are reluctant to pass along their knowledge, and the supply of domestic materials and papermaking tools is limited. It seems part of the solution to these problems is to sell inexpensive machine-made paper for everyday uses, hobbies, and crafts, and to use the finer handmade paper for more luxurious or serious endeavors.

Ultimately, demand drives the industry. With encouragement and patronage, well-informed consumers can help keep the tradition of handmade paper alive.[8]

In fact, paper continues to play a significant role in many festivals and rituals. For the Star Ritual, held in July, people write wishes on strips of *washi* and tie them to bamboo branches. On Children's Day, paper streamers shaped like carp are made from *washi*. The entranceways of shrines are often lined with rows of paper lanterns. Even fireworks are made from *washi*.

CHAPTER 3

A Brief History of Washi for Writing and Art

Before the invention of paper as we know it, ancient cultures wrote on other substrates such as clay, wood, slate, and animal-skin–based parchment. The first papers were made by hand using strips of silk fibers or plant fibers such as flax, hemp, or papyrus grass laid across one another and pounded into sheets. The result was a very strong substrate, but with an uneven surface, especially at the edges of the sheets. Also, when used in scrolls, repeated rolling and unrolling often caused the sheets to come apart, typically along vertical lines.

In 105 CE, an official in China's Emperor Ho Ti's imperial court, Ts'ai Lun, is said to have invented a forerunner of modern paper when he broke open the bark from a mulberry tree, separated it into fibers, then pounded them into a thick pulp. He spread the pulp onto a screen, submerged it in a vat of water, and pulled it out, discovering the fibers had knitted themselves together into a thin layer that dried into a sheet. The paper was called *Ts'ai ko-shi*, meaning "distinguished Ts'ai's paper." This so-called "first paper" differed from past iterations in that the plant material was broken down through maceration before the paper was pressed. This process produces a much more even surface with no natural weakness in the material, so it lasts a long time without tearing.

Circa 600 CE, papermaking spread westward along the Silk Road through Asia. It wasn't until the thirteenth century that knowledge of papermaking reached Europe.

The period of 1300 through 1800 represents the rise and decline of handmade papermaking as a major industry in Europe. During the late 1700s, traditional methods were still in use in many mills. However, after 1800, the process changed rapidly with the adoption of the papermaking machine—the Hollander beater—as well as the use of chlorine bleach, rosin, alum, and wood-pulp fibers.

England began making large amounts of paper in the late fifteenth century and supplied the American colonies with paper for many years. In 1690, the first US papermill was built in Rittenhouse Town, Pennsylvania. At first, American mills used shredded rags and old clothes as sources for papermaking. However, as the demand for paper grew, the mills changed to using fiber from trees, because wood was less expensive and more abundant than cloth.

Handmade papermaking schools began to appear in the United States in the 1970s, and it was around this time that handmade paper began to be popularized as an artform. The process used is similar to that of Japan in that a mold is submerged manually into a vat of dispersed pulp, but the molds are different. A Western mold has a rigid screen adhered to it or a set of two screens that one must hold together when dipping into pulp, whereas the Japanese mold, or *sugeta*, has a flexible, removeable bamboo screen.

CHAPTER 4

The Components of Washi and Kami-ito, and How to Make Them

Components and General Process

There are three kinds of *washi* (handmade paper) made in Japan, and they are derived from the inner bark of three native plants. *Kozo* (*Broussonetia papyrifera*), *mitsumata* (*Edgeworthia chrysantha*), or *gampi* (*Diplomorpha sikokiana*) fibers create strong, soft, crisp, and lightweight paper.

Kozo fibers are used in about ninety percent of the washi made today. They are the most robust of the three because they are especially long. *Mitsumata* is used to make a creamy-hued, firm paper, whereas *gampi washi* is pearly and somewhat translucent. Both mitsumata and gampi are insect-resistant, a natural plant defense against potential predators. Because it is difficult to cultivate, gampi shrubs are located in the wild—in the mountainous, warm regions of Japan—making this type of paper rare and expensive. It is sometimes referred to as *silk tissue*.

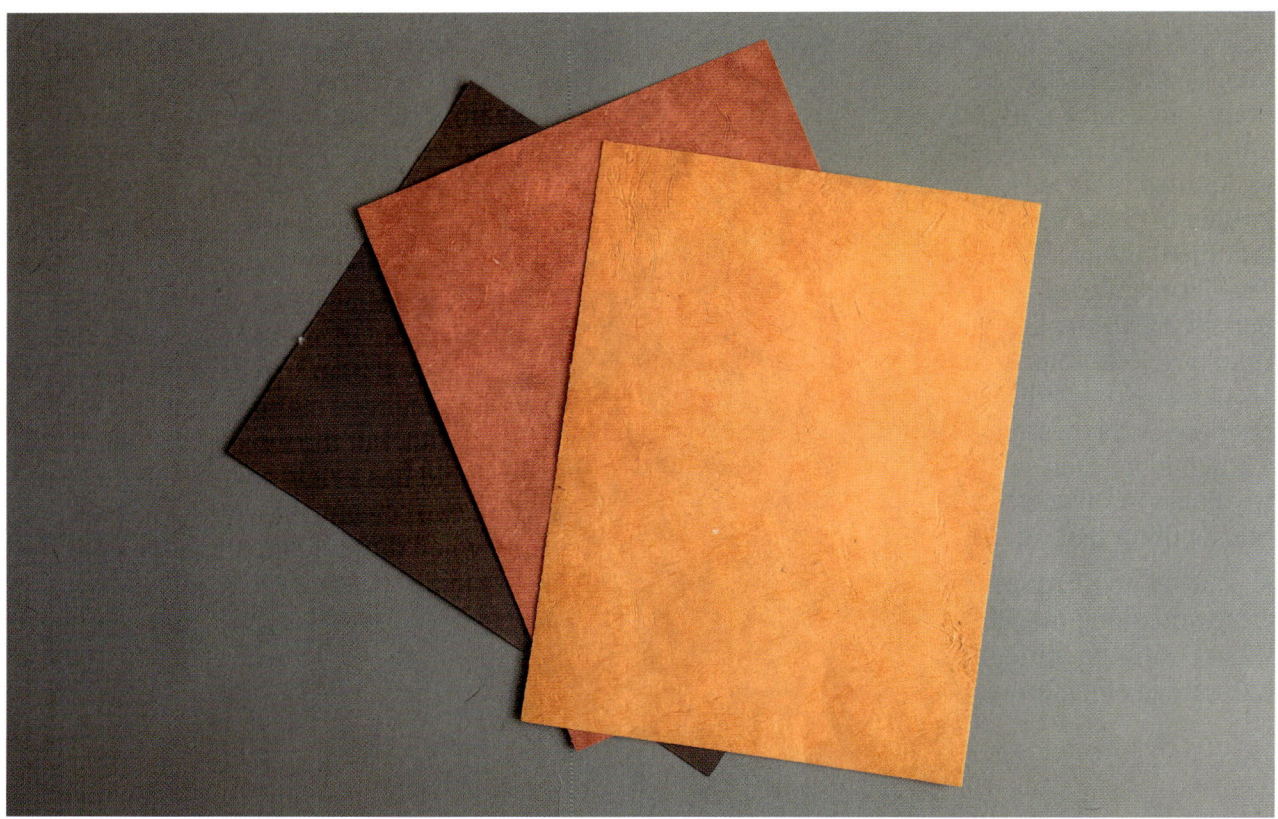

Naturally dyed purchased *washi. Photo courtesy of Nate Castner.*

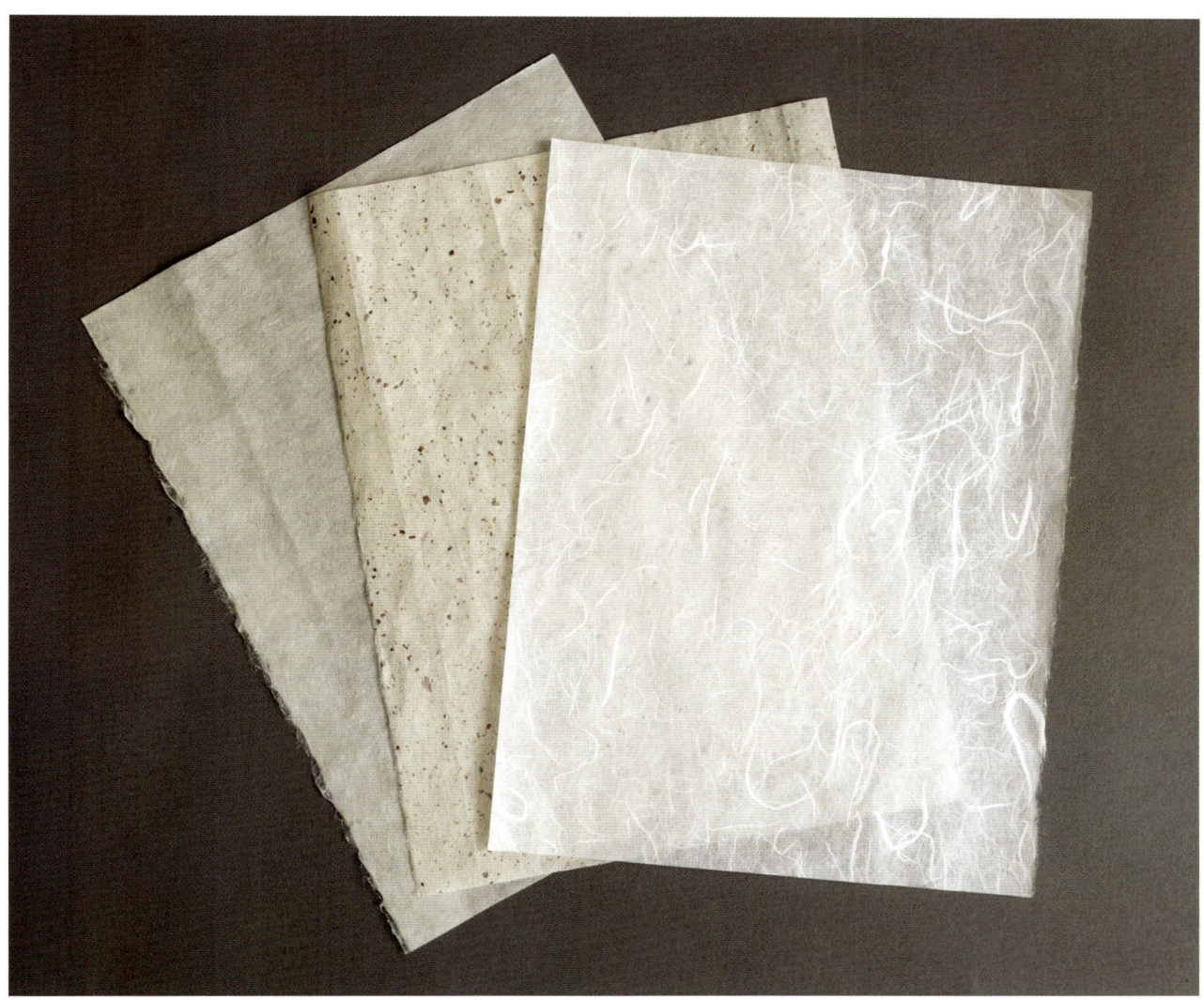

Purchased *washi. Photo courtesy of Nate Castner.*

Traditionally, the making of washi was a seasonal process. Most of the papermakers were farmers who planted kozo in addition to their regular crops. The best washi was made during the cold winter months, which coincided with the season when farmers could not work in their fields and icy water running through their villages was free of impurities (which, if present, could discolor the fibers).

During the manufacturing process, the long fibers of these three shrubs tend to ride up on each other, creating tiny layers of air, making the paper *appear* delicate, but in actuality such paper is hard to rip or tear.

Forming washi is labor-intensive. It involves many steps and relies on the keen skill and knowledge of seasoned papermakers. Moreover, there are strikingly diverse ways in which the steps are executed, beginning with the raw ingredients used. Regional differences in climate, water sources, fiber characteristics, available tools, and local tradition all play a role in how washi is produced.

In general, however, the steps used to make washi are fairly standard. Here, I refer to making washi with kozo. First, the bark is harvested in the fall, and bundles of kozo sticks are steamed, stripped of their outer bark, and the inner bark strips are hung to dry. These are then soaked in cold water for at least eight hours, until the inner bark softens.

The bark is then boiled with wood ash or soda ash for two hours and rinsed in cold water. Next, the bark is beaten with a wooden mallet until it looks like cooked oatmeal. Next, one adds a vegetable mucilage, or glue, called *neri* (derived from a hibiscus, *Abelmoschus manihot*) to help the fibers adhere to one another. This mixture is then formed into sheets using a hinged mold, or *sugeta*, which is dipped in a water-filled wooden tub. The fibers are rocked on the *sugeta* screen in an up-and-down or side-to-side direction. The *neri* keeps the fibers suspended in the water, which allows the formation of a uniform layer and thin layers to be built up, if desired. This process of forming sheets is known as *nagashisuki*.

Next, the sheets are stacked on top of one another and pressed for up to ten hours to remove excess water. Each sheet is then pulled from the pile and placed on a board or metal sheet, brushed flat, and left in the sun to dry. Last, the paper is stored for as long as two years, during which the fibers settle and increase the bonds between them, thus giving the washi greater strength and smoothness.

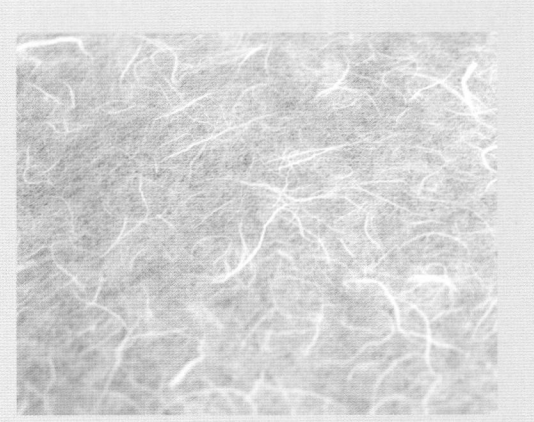

WHERE TO BUY WASHI

Among the sources of high-quality washi, shops featuring specialty papers are wonderful because they often have experts who can educate you. The following websites are among those that offer a wide variety of washi. I've listed a few of my favorite papers that I often order.

- Washi Arts (washiarts.com): Ogunigami heritage *washi*

- Paper Connection (paperconnection.com): Nishinouchi Shifuyoushi-N-0007

- Hiromi Paper (hiromipaper.com): HM-35 Senka-shi Thin, Nara Natural Dyed Papers, HM-56 Yukyu-shi Medium, R-012 Sekishu Medium roll

Safety Note: Because cooking the bark produces a strong odor, it is best to do this step in a well-ventilated room (i.e., with all doors and windows open and/or with multiple fans) or outside on an electric burner.

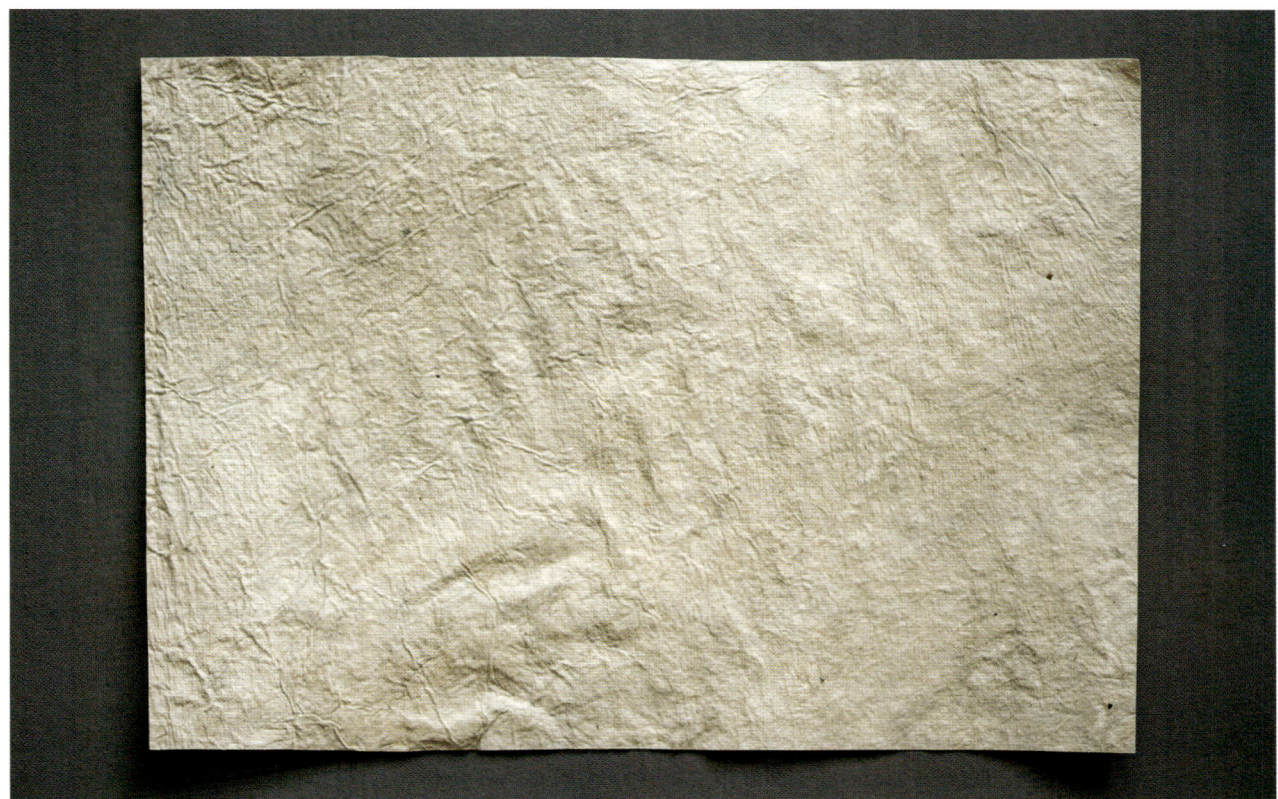

Homemade Thai kozo paper. *Photo courtesy of Nate Castner.*

Japanese kozo bark for papermaking can be hard to find and, when you do find it, is expensive. A cheaper alternative is Thai kozo, which is identical botanically to Japanese kozo. The difference between the two results from Thailand's warmer climate, which changes the characteristics of the plant fiber. The Japanese fiber is more lustrous and, when dry, it has a yellow-green tinge, whereas the Thai fiber is tan.

HOW TO MAKE *WASHI*

Don't expect to make the thinnest of thin, nearly translucent, flat paper matching what you can purchase. The process of making exquisite washi is even more labor-intensive, calls for additional equipment, and requires hours and hours of preparation—and experience—even before pulping. The instructions included here will give you an idea of how much work goes into the creation of perfect or even near-perfect paper.

In my opinion, pulping—or macerating—is the hardest part of this project. If you don't have much upper body strength and can't get friends and/or family to help, you can use a dedicated-to-crafts blender. Beware, however, that using a craft blender for longer than five short bursts chops the fibers and thus is not ideal; its use actually *defeats* the purpose of using kozo, with its long fibers that provide strength and durability. If you opt for using a blender, place a small handful of cooked and rinsed fiber into the blender with two cups of water and blend for one minute. If your blender won't churn, turn it off *immediately*. Try again with less fiber or more water or both. Otherwise, you'll burn out the motor on your blender.

- 8 oz. Thai kozo (see Sources list)

- ⅛ tsp. *neri* (mine is from hiromipaper.com)

- 1.5 oz. soda ash (see Sources list)

- 1 2-c. measuring cup

- 1 large wooden spoon dedicated to crafting, a wooden dowel, or a paint stir-stick

- 1 pair of rubber gloves

- 1 pair of safety glasses

- 1 N-95 mask

- 1 10-qt. or larger cooking pot (stainless steel or enamel) (I use a dedicated 15.5-qt. lobster pot.)

- 1 large strainer, such as a laundry basket with small holes

- 1 Japanese *sugeta* (mine is from carriagehousepaper.com) or Western paper mold (mine is from arnoldgrummer.com)

- 1 wooden or rubber mallet or hammer (or a meat tenderizer)

- 1 10-gal. plastic mixing tub, 28" × 20" × 6" deep

- 1 1-c. glass jar with lid

- Pellon heavy stabilizer cut into sheets slightly larger than your mold and dampened, or a glass window or glass sheet on your work table, or a Formica sheet. It must be at least as large as your sugeta or Western paper mold.

- 1 sponge

- 1 piece of window mesh netting as large as your sugeta or mold

- 1 soft brush (I use a flat hake paintbrush)

- 1 mesh strainer bag (I use a 14" × 14" nut-milk bag)

INSTRUCTIONS

1. Soak the bark for at least 8 hours—preferably, 72 hours—in cold water. Change the water every 8 hours. After soaking, the fiber will be very soft and can be pulled apart easily. I like to divide each fiber length into thin strips at this point.

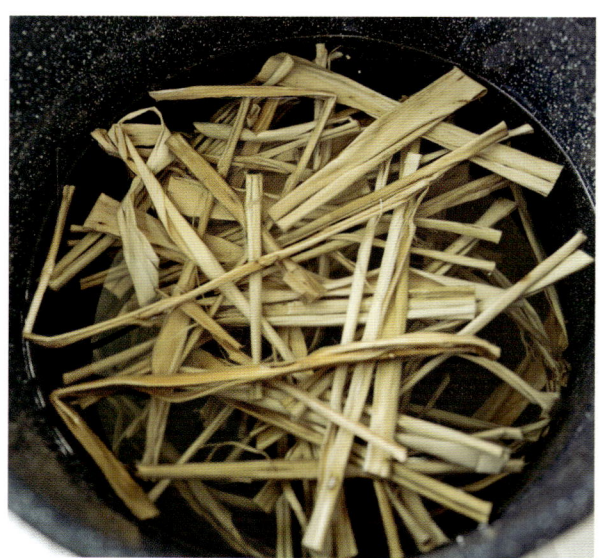

Step 1: Soaking raw kozo. *Step photos courtesy of Nate Castner.*

2 In the large pot, bring 7 quarts of water to a boil.

3 Because you will be using caustic soda ash in this step, it is *important* that you wear rubber gloves, safety glasses, and a mask when handling it. Direct skin or eye contact, or inhalation of the powder or crystals, can produce irritation, rash, and sometimes burns. Add the soda ash to 1 cup of hot water and stir until it is dissolved.

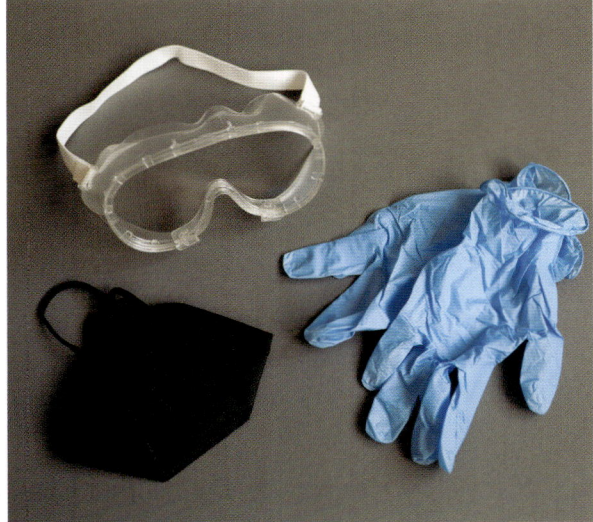

Step 3: Protective safety equipment.

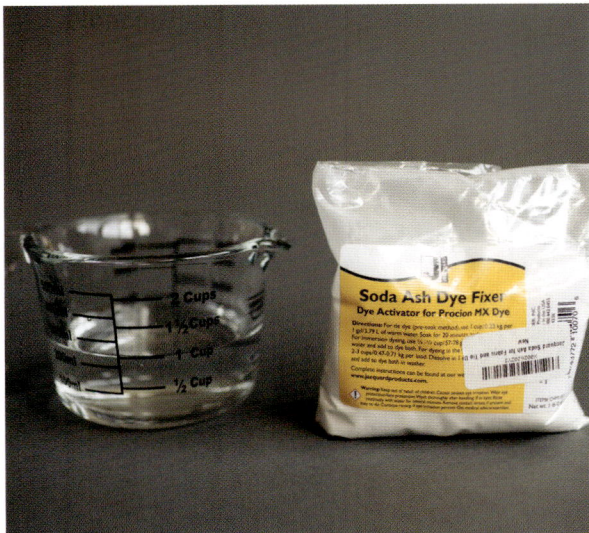

Step 3: Add soda ash to water.

4 When dissolved, carefully pour the soda ash solution into the large pot. You may now remove your safety glasses and mask.

5 Add the soaked fiber and use the craft-dedicated wooden spoon to submerge all of it. Angle the lid of the pot so that steam can escape, and simmer for 2 to 3 hours, stirring every 30 minutes. Let cool.

6 The kozo is fully cooked when it comes apart easily. Drain the water from the pot. Transfer the fiber from the pot to the laundry basket and rinse it with cold water until the rinse water shows no evidence of lingering ash. (The fiber should no longer be slippery to the touch.) If doing this step outside, you can use a hose to rinse the fibers. If you haven't already done so, tear the kozo into thin strips.

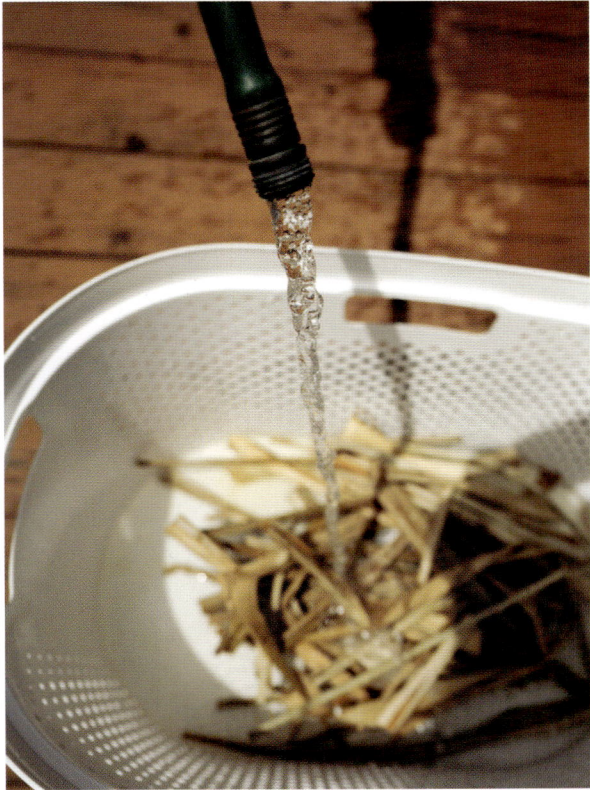

Step 6: Using a hose to wash the cooked kozo in a plastic laundry basket.

The Components of Washi and Kami-ito | 2 7

7. Grab a fistful of fiber at a time, place it on a hard surface, and, using the mallet or hammer, beat the fiber into a pulp. I pound the fiber for a few minutes, then rest, then continue beating it, and, when pulped, set it aside. I grab more handfuls of fiber and repeat. If you have friends or family willing to help out, go ahead and enlist them! If you must, use a blender, but note that doing so will affect the quality of your washi. (See page 25.)

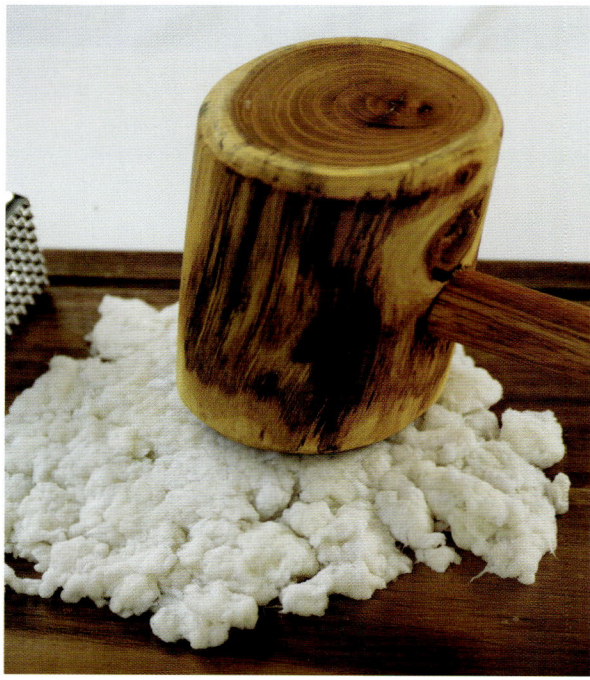

Step 7: Macerating the kozo to a pulp using a wooden mallet.

8. When all the fiber has been rendered to pulp, place a tablespoon of pulp in a jar of water and shake it well. If there are no clumps, then the pulp is ready.

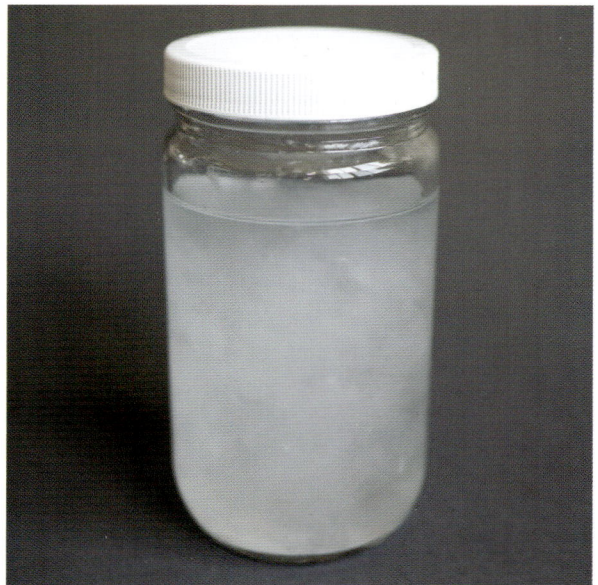

Step 8: Ensuring the pulp is primed (no clumps) and ready for use.

9. Fill the mixing tub halfway with water. Place 2 cups of beaten pulp into the tub, along with ⅛ teaspoon of *neri*. Stir the contents of the tub with your hand to disperse the fibers.

10. Place all pieces of your mold, either Japanese or Western, into the water, holding them tightly together. Dip the mold edge-first into the pulp, trapping some pulp on the mold. Lift the mold out of the water.

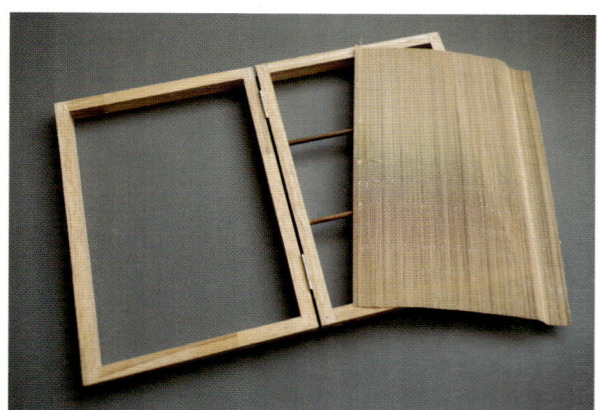

Step 10: A Japanese *sugeta*.

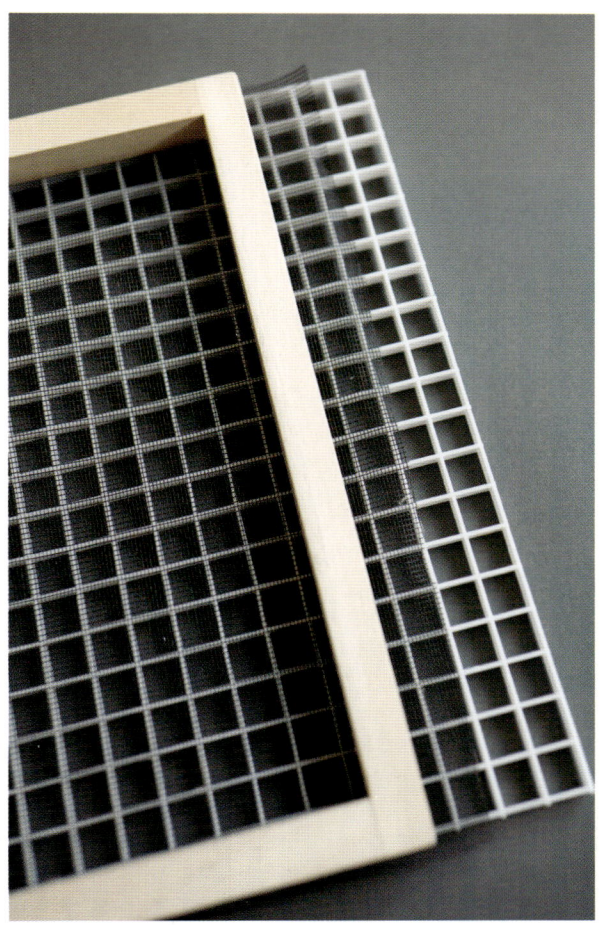

Step 10: A Western mold.

11 Hold the mold level and rock it gently side to side to let the fibers intertwine and settle. Tip the mold over the tub and let the water drain off. Then remove the top of the sugeta or mold and place the mesh netting over the paper sheet. Use the sponge to soak up more water by pressing it all over the netting, squeezing the sponge dry as you go.

12 You are now ready to *couch* the sheet. Couching (pronounced *kooching*) is the process of getting the wet sheet of washi off the mold. To do this, turn the mold over and *press it firmly* onto the *wet* Pellon sheet. Now you are ready to remove the screen.

Alternatively, press the paper sheet on the mold directly onto a window, a sheet of glass, or a sheet of Formica. Run the sponge over the mold to release the paper and lift the sugeta or mold off. Let completely dry, then peel off the Pellon, window, glass, or Formica. Burnish the paper to the glass or Formica by lightly stroking it all over with a soft brush.

13 Repeat this process, beginning at Step 10, to make more sheets of washi. Couch them next to one another.

14 If you wish to make crinkled paper, or momigami, do so now following the directions below.

15 Wash your mold thoroughly. To discard the water containing the pulp, pour both through a strainer and place leftover pulp in a container. Freeze it to save, dispose of it, or compost it. Your water will be clear and can be poured down a drain.

Different kinds of pulp, such as kozo and abaca, can be combined, so your saved pulp can help you experiment.

16 Your washi can be used to make *kami-ito*, or paper yarn.

HOW TO MAKE *KONJAC* PASTE AND CRUMPLED PAPER (*MOMIGAMI*)

To make your *washi* more textured and more waterproof, you can apply *konjac* paste to it.

— SUPPLIES —

- 1 tsp. *konjac* (also called *konyaku*) powder (one source is paperconnection.com)

- 2 c. room-temperature water

- 1 wooden spoon

- 1 3"-wide paintbrush

- 1 dry *washi* sheet, size depending on your project

- 1 plastic sheet large enough to protect work area

INSTRUCTIONS

1. Dissolve 1 teaspoon of *konjac* powder in 2 cups of room-temperature water by adding a little bit of powder at a time, stirring constantly. Continue to stir for 20 minutes to prevent lumps. Stir occasionally for the next couple of hours as the mixture begins to solidify. The paste is ready when it is thick and smooth, and the particles have dissolved.

2. Use the paintbrush to apply paste to both sides of the paper. If your washi is delicate and begins to tear when you apply the paste, dilute the paste with some water, stirring constantly to incorporate, until you have the right consistency.

3. Crumple each sheet of paper by squeezing it into a loose ball. Then, open each sheet and rub your hands against both sides of it. Flatten the washi, stretch it gently, and lay it flat to dry. It will have a bumpy surface.

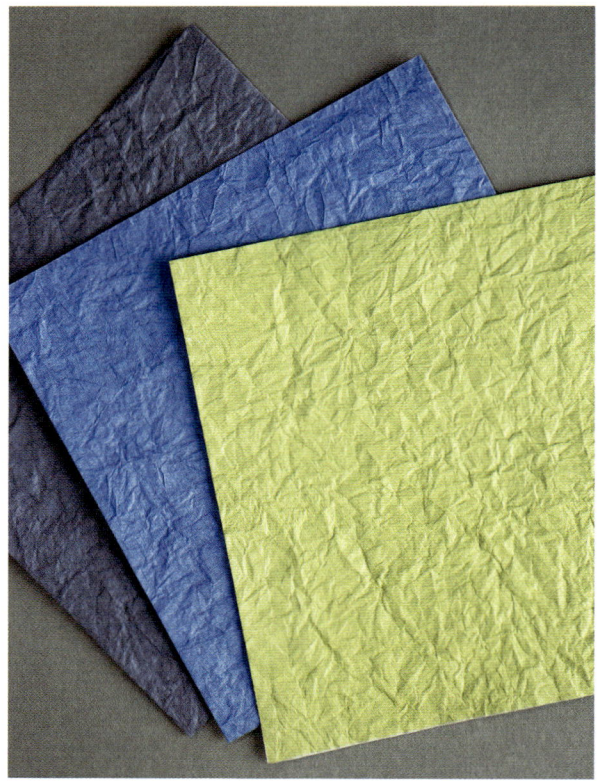

Momigami. *Photo courtesy of Nate Castner.*

HOW TO MAKE KAMI-ITO

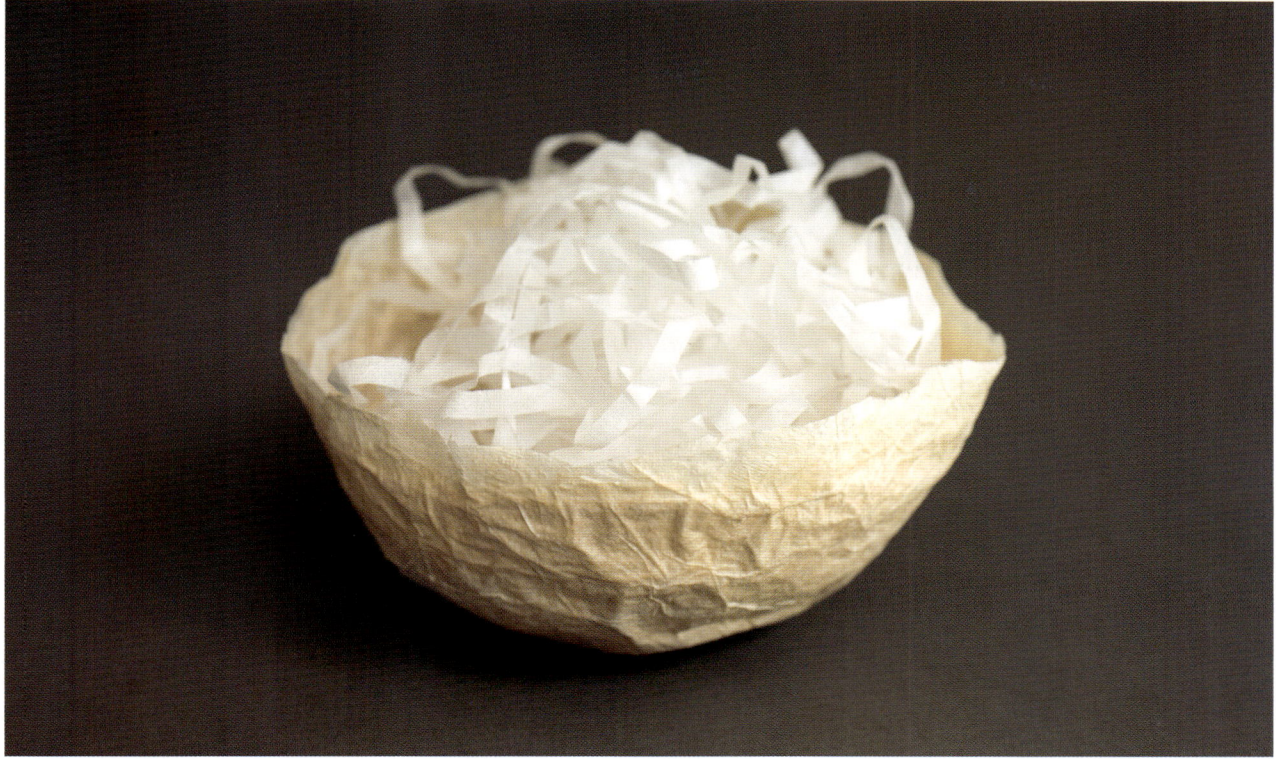

Paper strips ready to be made into kami-ito. *Photo courtesy of Nate Castner.*

The best-made *kami-ito*, or paper yarn, is a complicated and time-consuming endeavor that has been perfected by experts who have practiced for many months or years. Here, I present the steps to follow to make *kami-ito*, but your results will not be as tight, smooth, and strong as that made by experts or machines. However, your paper yarn should work well for the how-to projects in this book.

If you are a beginner, I recommend using a half sheet of 24"-by-36" washi.

In addition to Japanese kozo, you can use Thai *unryu* kozo. In fact, misted and twisted paper of almost any kind (for example, new or used coffee filters, used tea bags, new tea bag paper, newspaper, magazine pages, and wrapping paper)—as long as it's lightweight—can be used to make *kami-ito* if you're very careful not to pull or twist too tightly when the paper is still damp. The advantage of using kozo is that it's strong and will withstand more easily the tugging needed for weaving, crochet, macrame, and knitting projects.

IF VIDEO IS YOUR THING

The process involved in making *kami-ito* is very complex. To get a better feel for the procedure, you can watch others making it. Go to youtube.com and, in the search bar, type "how to make kami-ito," "how to make Japanese paper yarn," or a similar description.

- 1 metal or plastic ruler

- 1 cutting mat

- 1 craft knife or rotary cutter

- 1 heavy stone, paperweight, or other small, heavy, clean object

- 1 fine-mist spray bottle filled with water

- 1 towel

- 1 drop spindle or spinning wheel

- 1 small bowl

- 1 bobbin or skewer

- 1 standard cinderblock (such as a 6" × 8" × 16" cored concrete block) or the back surface of a section of wall-to-wall carpet similar in size (6" × 16")

- 1 sheet of washi, 21" × 2" (cut in half vertically), appprox. 25 g (see "Where to Buy Washi" or use your own handmade washi)

- several marbles, smooth pebbles, or flat marbles (vase fillers)

- small container of hydrated methylcellulose glue powder (take care to follow manufacturer's directions)

INSTRUCTIONS

1 Fold the washi in half lengthwise. Next, fold each long side toward the initial fold, but in the opposite direction, leaving a ½-inch overhang on each end. You should have a W-shaped folded sheet of washi.

Step 1: W-shaped folded sheet of washi. *Step photos courtesy of Nate Castner.*

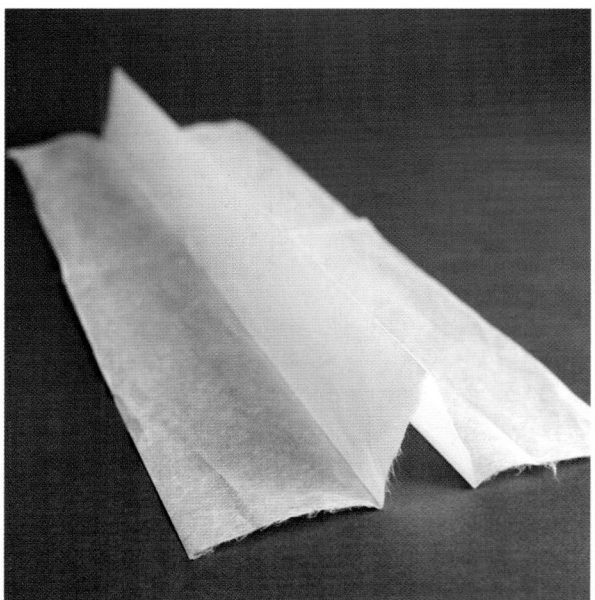

Step 1: W-shaped folded sheet of washi.

2. Place the sheet in the center of a cutting mat and set the rock or other heavy object on one end of the washi so the paper doesn't move when you start to cut it. I draw ¼-inch or ½-inch (your preference) cutting lines in pencil, but you don't have to. Using a craft knife or rotary cutter, first trim the uneven edge opposite from the rock so you have a clean, straight edge

3. Cut the washi into ¼-inch-wide strips, but stop just past the beginning of the ½-inch extension. Apply enough pressure to cut through all the layers of the folded paper, especially the inner folded edges.

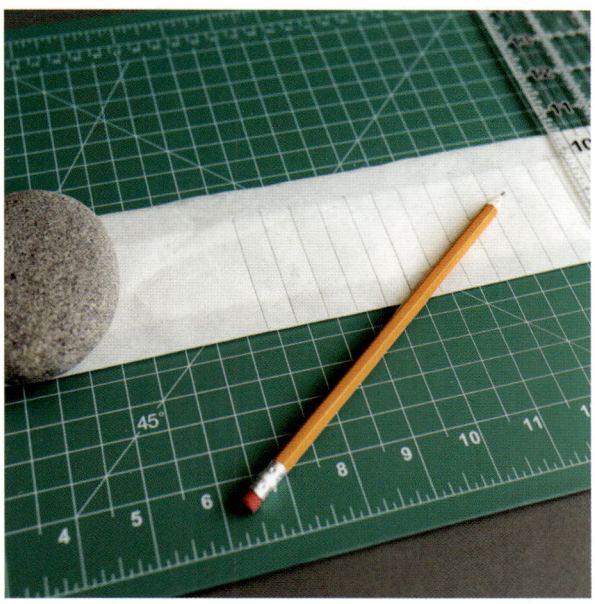

Step 2: Using a rock or other heavy object to keep the washi stable while drawing cutting lines and trimming the rough edge.

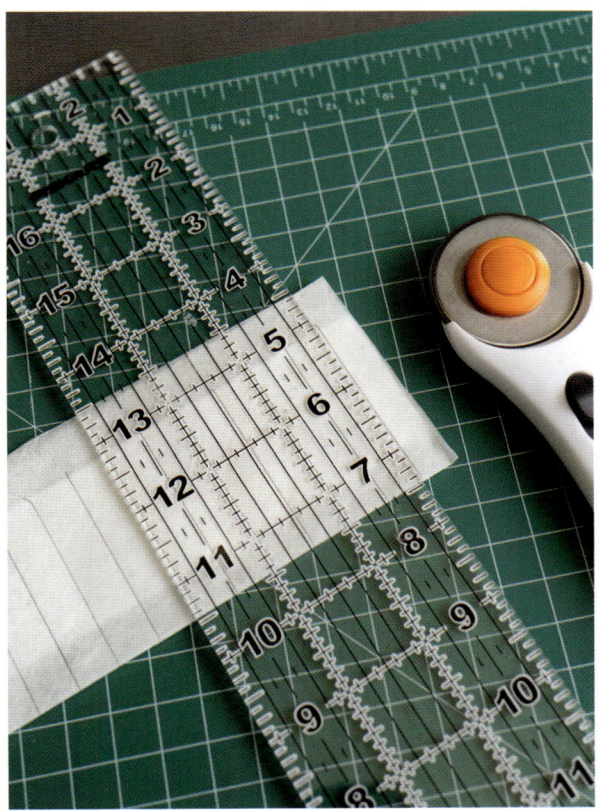

Step 3: Trimmed edge preparatory to cutting the washi.

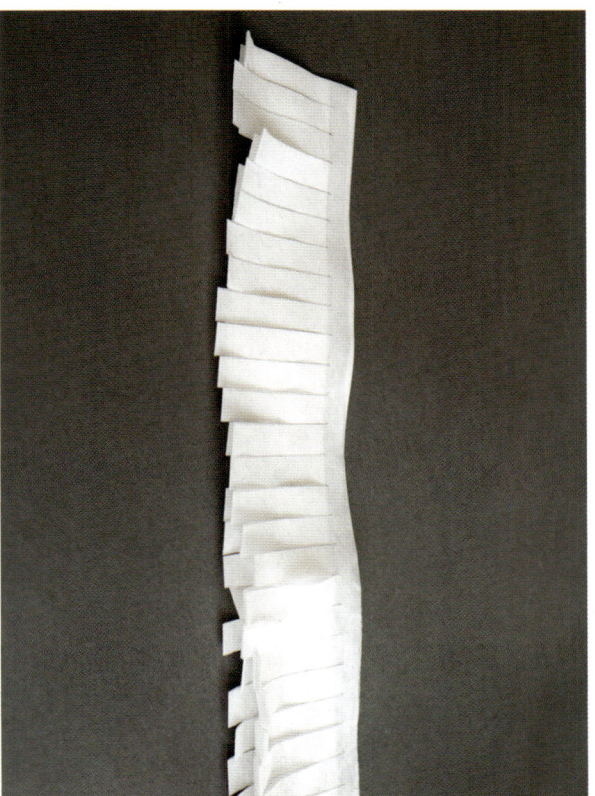

4. Use the fine-mist sprayer to dampen the still-folded cut washi. Place the still-folded cut washi on the towel and roll it up. Let it sit 1 to 3 minutes. Unroll the towel; if the strips are too wet and translucent, do not touch them because they may fall apart. Let them dry out a bit while still remaining on the towel.

5. Remove the washi from the towel and unfold it carefully.

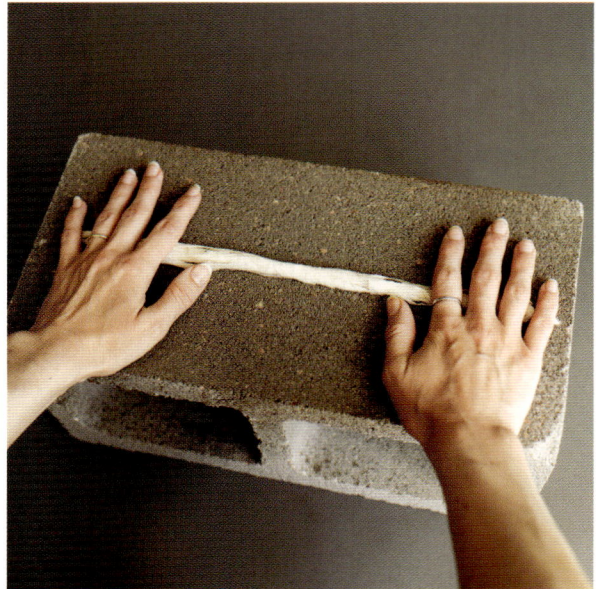

Step 6: Rolling the damp washi.

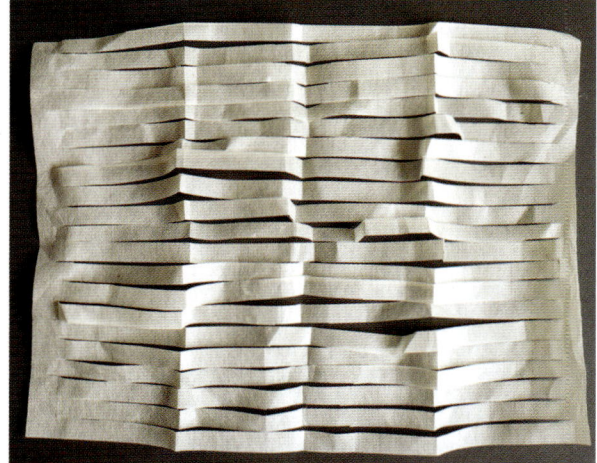

Step 5: The unrolled, unfolded washi, removed from the towel.

7. Unroll the bundle carefully.

6. Gather the uncut edges to form a long bundle. Place it on a cinder block, or other rough surface (such as carpet backing) and roll it gently back and forth about 5 times. Unroll the sheet and shake it out to straighten the strips. Separate any tangles by tugging the bundle sharply by holding both ends. Put the bundle back on the cinder block and roll again until the strips begin to twist. This takes about 10 minutes.

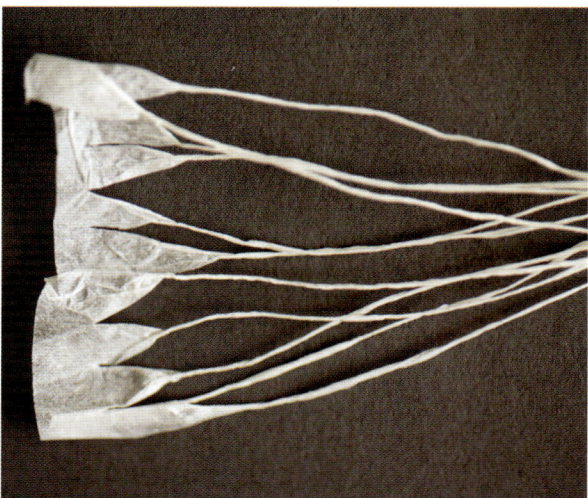

Step 7: Partially unrolled bundle.

8 At one end of the top or bottom of the bundle, tear off a strand carefully. Move to the other side of the bundle, skip the next flat side, and tear the second flat side. This keeps the kami-ito connected. Move back to your starting side of the bundle, skip the next flat side, and tear the second flat side. Continue tearing one side then the other in this manner, keeping the kami-ito in one long strand.

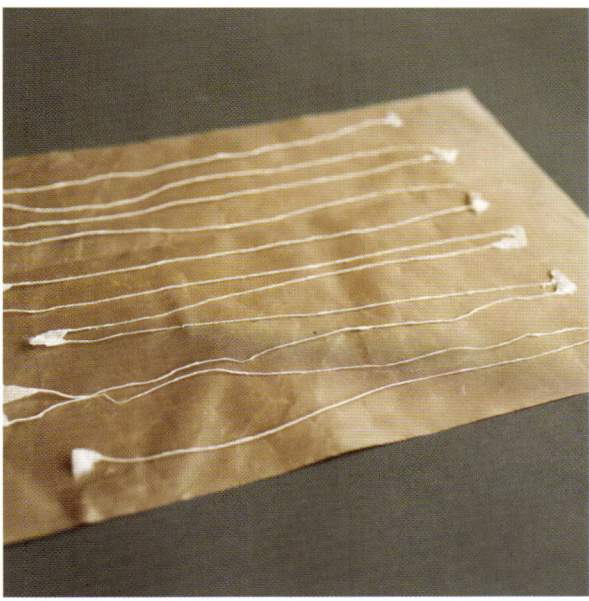

Step 8: Separating the strips after unrolling the bundle.

9 The flat bits, or attached areas, are called joints. Twist all the joints using your thumb and index finger so that you have one long strand. As you finish twisting the yarn, place it loosely in a bowl with clean pebbles, marbles, or other small, smooth objects. I use flat glass marbles. The marbles help to keep the kami-ito from becoming tangled.

10 Place one end of the yarn on a drop spindle and wind it onto the spindle. Spin as usual, letting the thread twist as it winds onto the spindle. If you don't have a spinning wheel or drop spindle,

use your forefinger and thumb to twist one length of the paper as you hold the end of that section taut. If the washi unfurls, add some hydrated methylcellulose to your fingers as you twist. Repeat with any stubborn sections until the methylcellulose holds the twist.

If you use the methylcellulose, the resulting kami-ito will be stiff, and therefore not ideal to work with, but suitable for most of the how-to projects in this book.

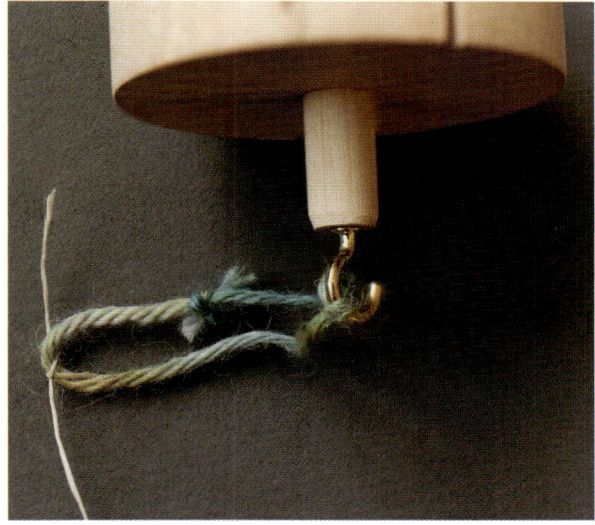

Step 10: Threading the twisted strips onto the spindle.

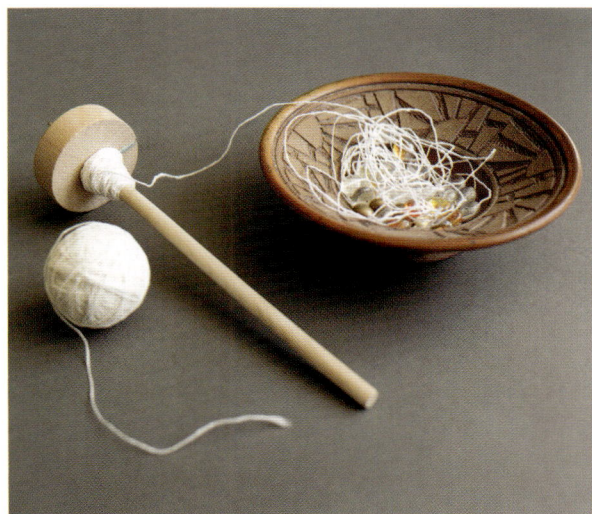

Step 10: Placing the damp strips in a bowl filled with glass marbles to keep them separated while spinning.

11 Now transfer the kami-ito by loosely winding it around a wooden bobbin or skewer that can withstand the heat of the steam of boiling water.

12 Hold the bobbin or skewer over a pot of boiling water for 20 seconds. When the kami-ito is slightly damp, remove it from the heat and wind it slowly into a ball or leave it as a skein.

WHERE TO PURCHASE KAMI-ITO

Because creating your own paper yarn is a bit of a challenge, consider treating yourself by buying it. The following websites are among those that offer wonderful kami-ito:

- Paper yarn or twine from Paperphine: paperphine.com
- Newspaper yarn from Paperuli: etsy.com/shop/paperuli
- Linen, nettle, bamboo, and pine yarns from orafabulousfibres.com

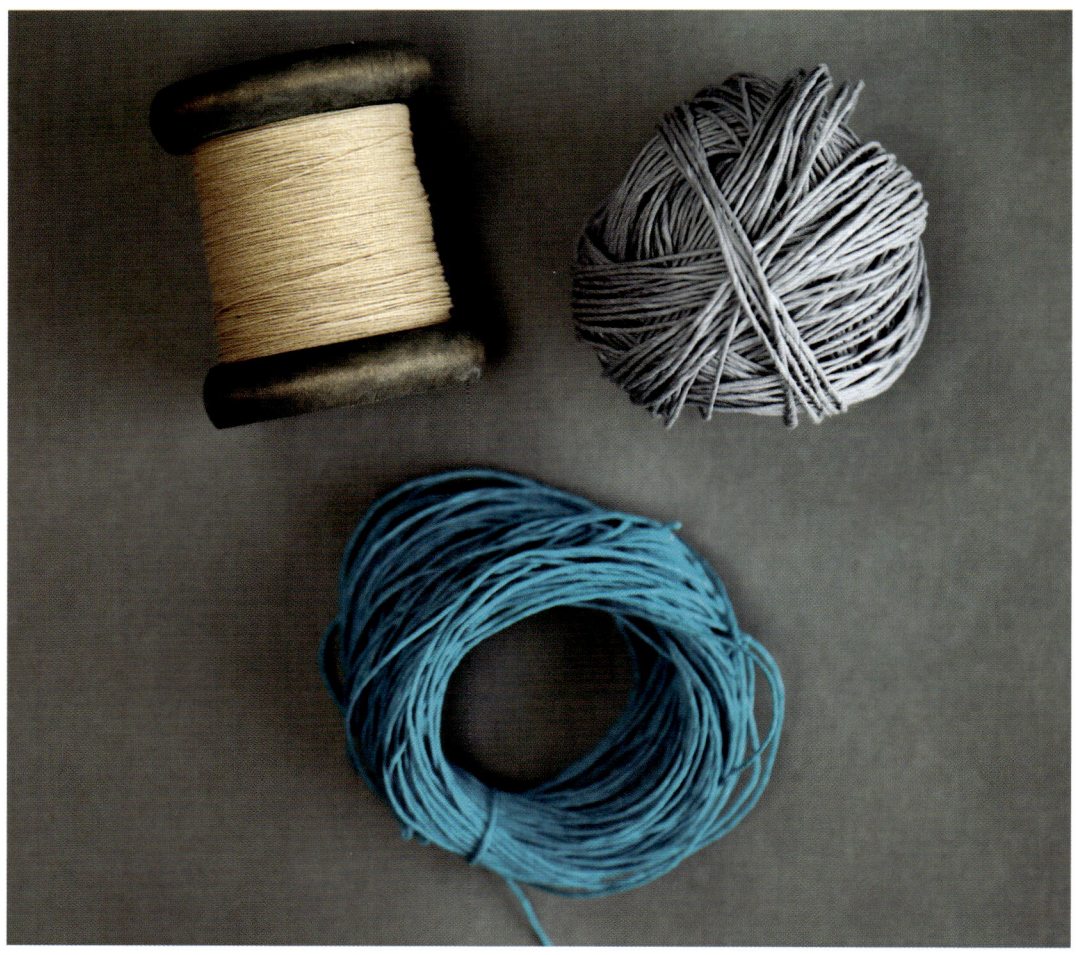

Kami-ito. *Photo courtesy of Nate Castner.*

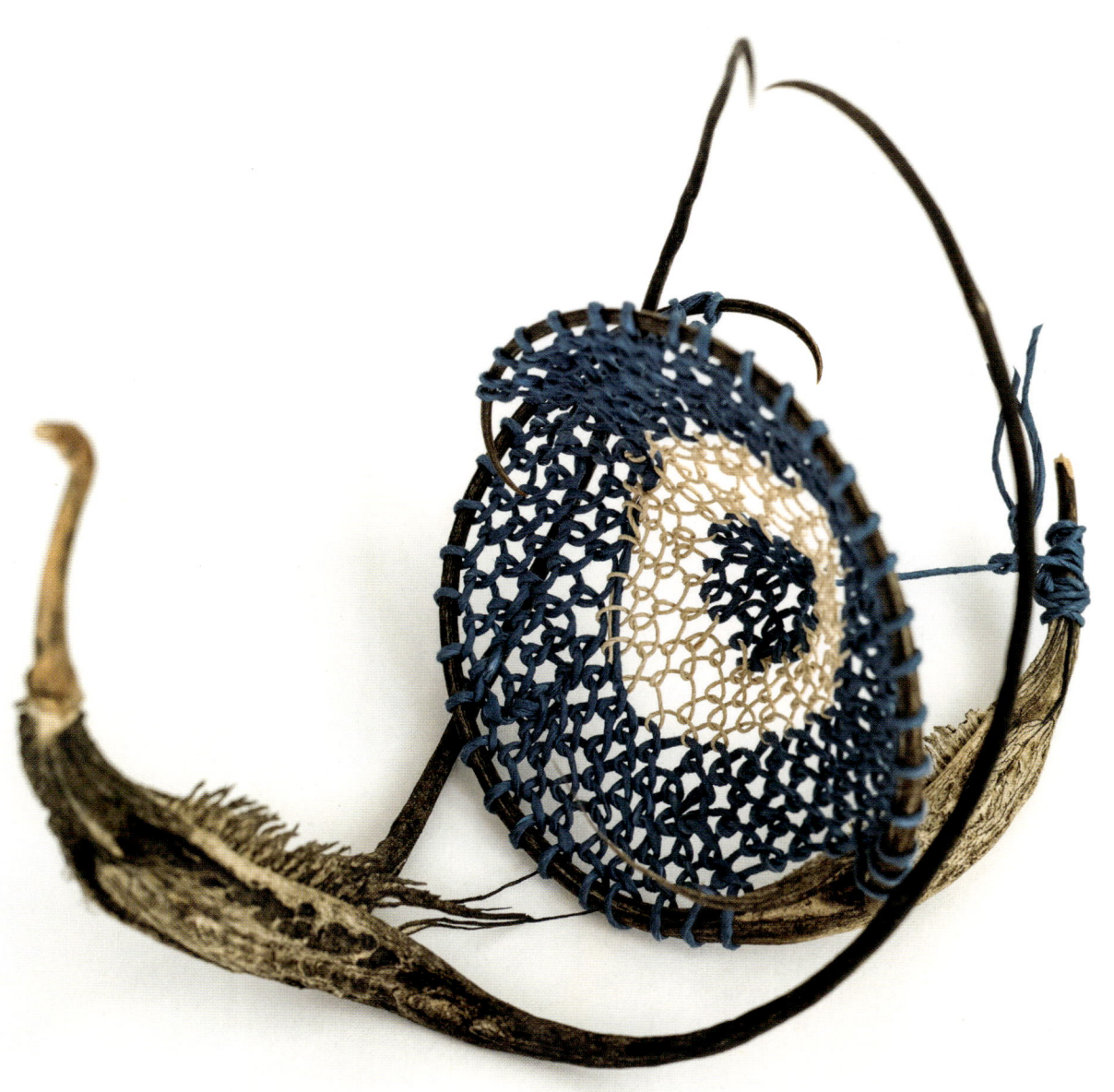

Carol Eaton. *Devil's Claw Pod Loop Weaving*, 2023. 7" × 6". Devil's claw pod, paper yarn. Handweaving. *Photo courtesy of Nate Castner.*

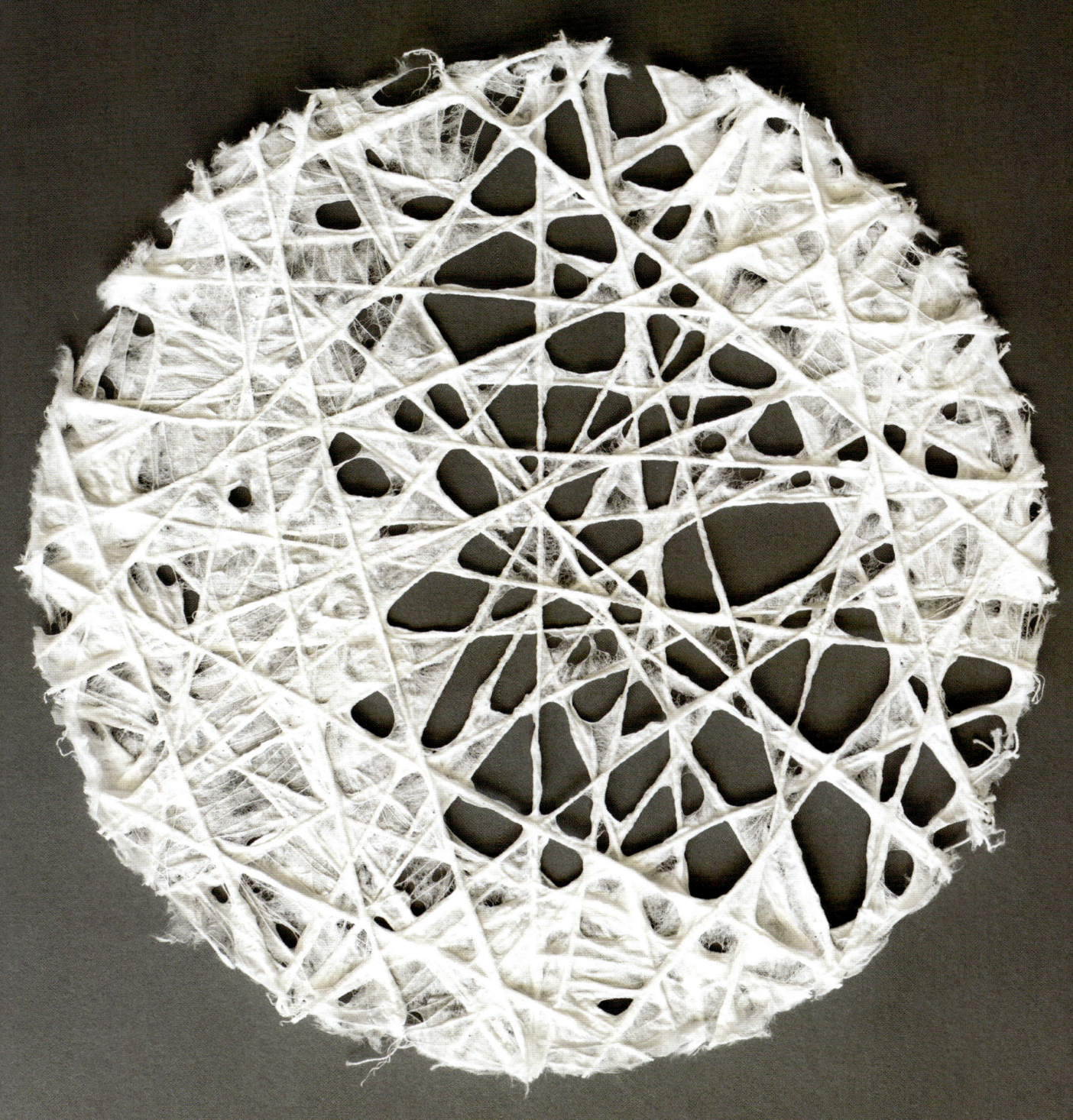

Pulped Paper Weaving by Jennifer Davies.
Photo courtesy of Nate Castner.

Pulped Paper Weaving

BY JENNIFER DAVIES | JENNIFERDAVIESHMP.COM

Skill Level: Intermediate

SUPPLIES

- 1 sheet of washi, 24" ×36"

- 600 yards *kami-ito*, any kind

- 1 plastic tub

- 1 wooden or plastic hoop, any size (I used a 14-inch hoop)

- double-sided tape

- thread, any kind (*optional*)

INSTRUCTIONS

1 Tear the washi into small pieces and soak it in a tub of water.

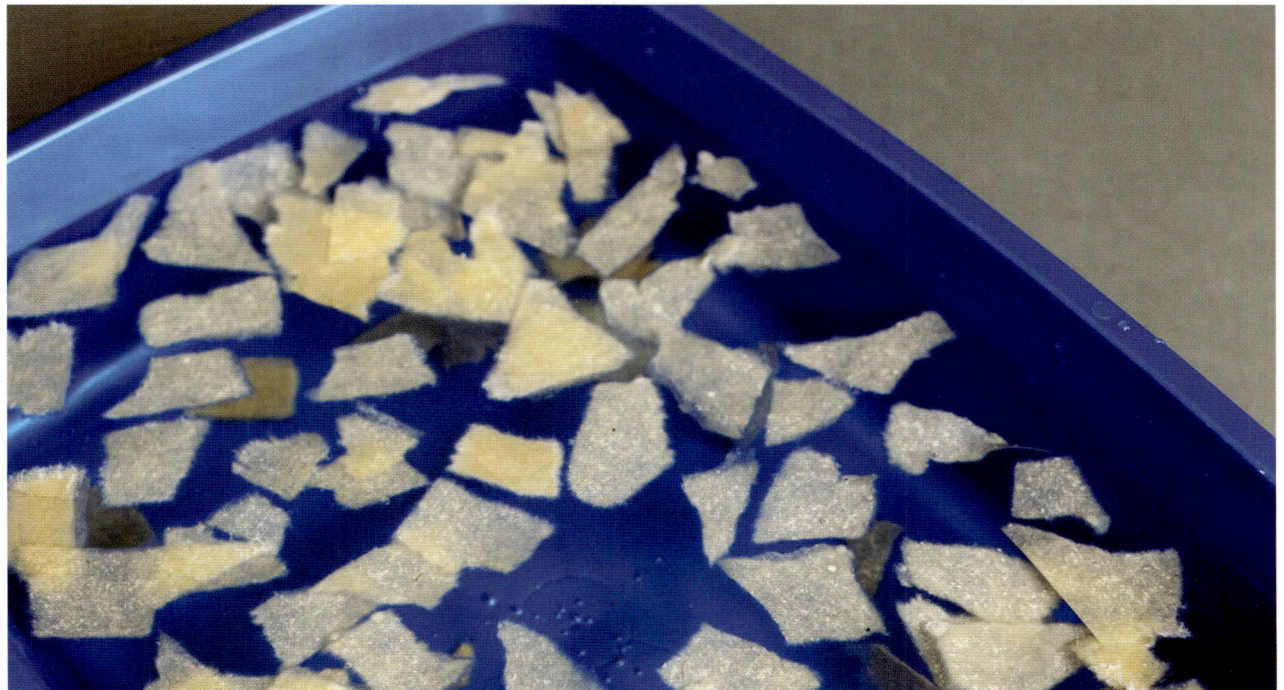

Step 1: Torn strips of *washi*, soaking in a tub of water. *Step photos courtesy of Nate Castner.*

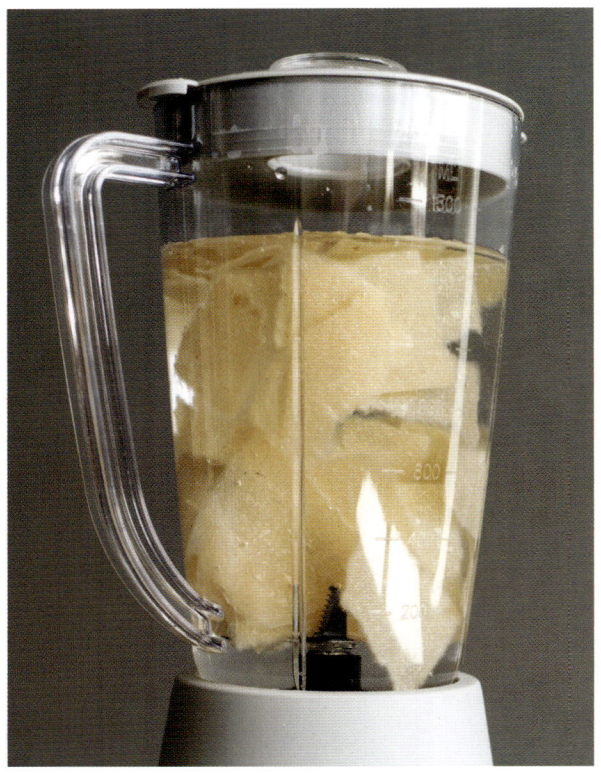

Step 2: Processing the torn paper in a blender.

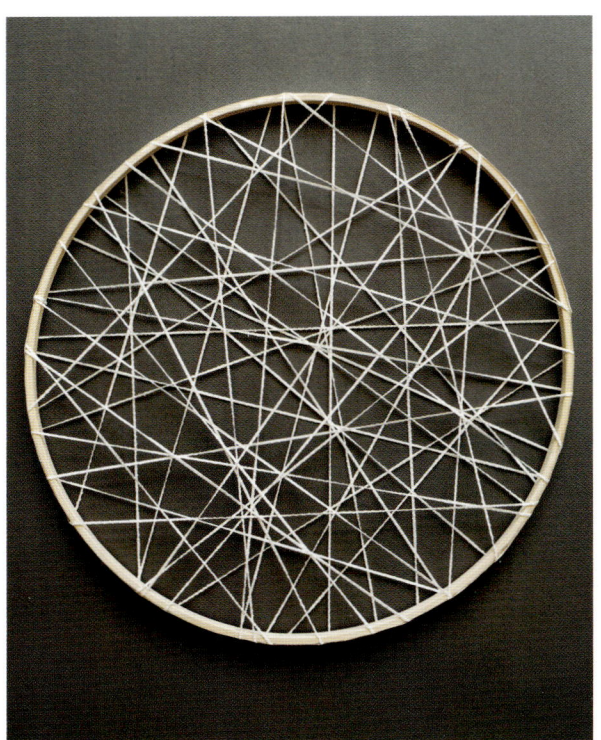

Step 5: *Kami-ito* wrapped around a wooden hoop, adhered to the sides of the hoop with double-sided tape.

2 Put a few pieces of the torn paper in a blender. Fill approximately two thirds of the blender with water. Blend for 10 to 15 seconds, or just long enough to make sure the *washi* is mushy. You might need to rearrange the contents of the blender a couple times to make sure they've broken down.

3 Pour the pulp into a big tub of water. You want there to be very little pulp to lots of water. A modest amount of pulp provides for a more transparent look. You can always add more pulp for a thicker finished look. Set this aside for now.

4 Secure a layer of double-sided tape along the outside of the hoop to keep the yarn in place.

5 Wrap the hoop with *kami-ito*, as shown in the photo.

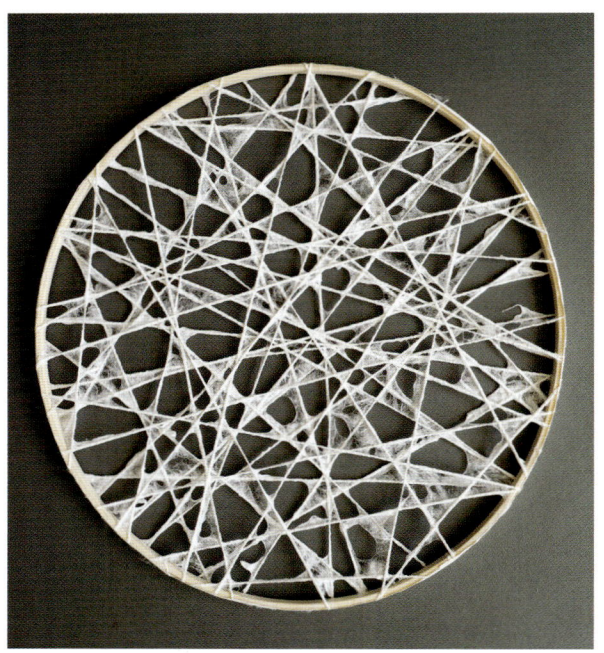

Step 6: The first dip of the hoop into the pulp.

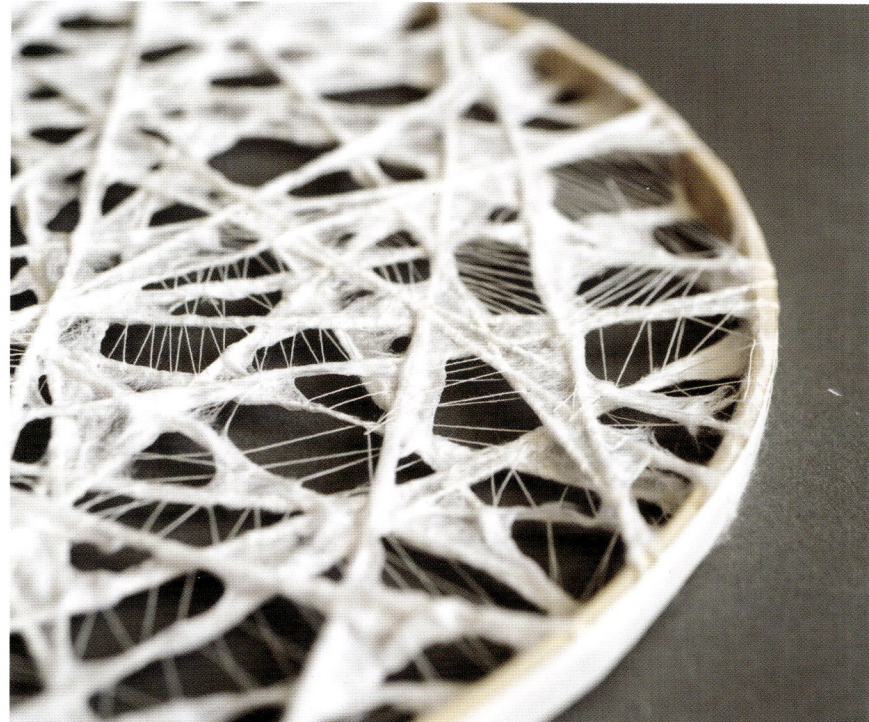

Step 8: Thread sewn around the *kami-ito* and pulp prior to a final dip.

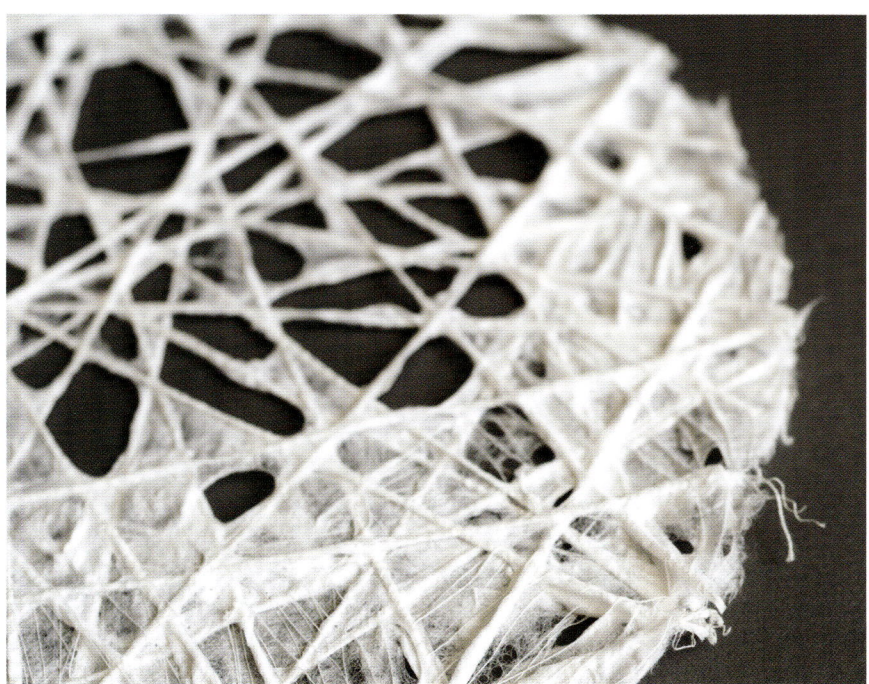

Step 9: Pulped paper construction cut from the hoop.

6. Dip the hoop into the pulp and water. The pulp from the first dip will look very transparent. However, as it dries, it will appear thicker and opaque.

7. Dip the hoop again—over all areas or specific areas only—to achieve a variety of opaque and transparent sections.

8. For this project, I did some extra sewing on the hoop using regular thread to make a tight web to which the pulp could stick, then dipped again. This step is optional.

9. Cut the *kami-ito*-and-pulp construction from the hoop. The edge can be made very clean or wispy. The choice is yours!

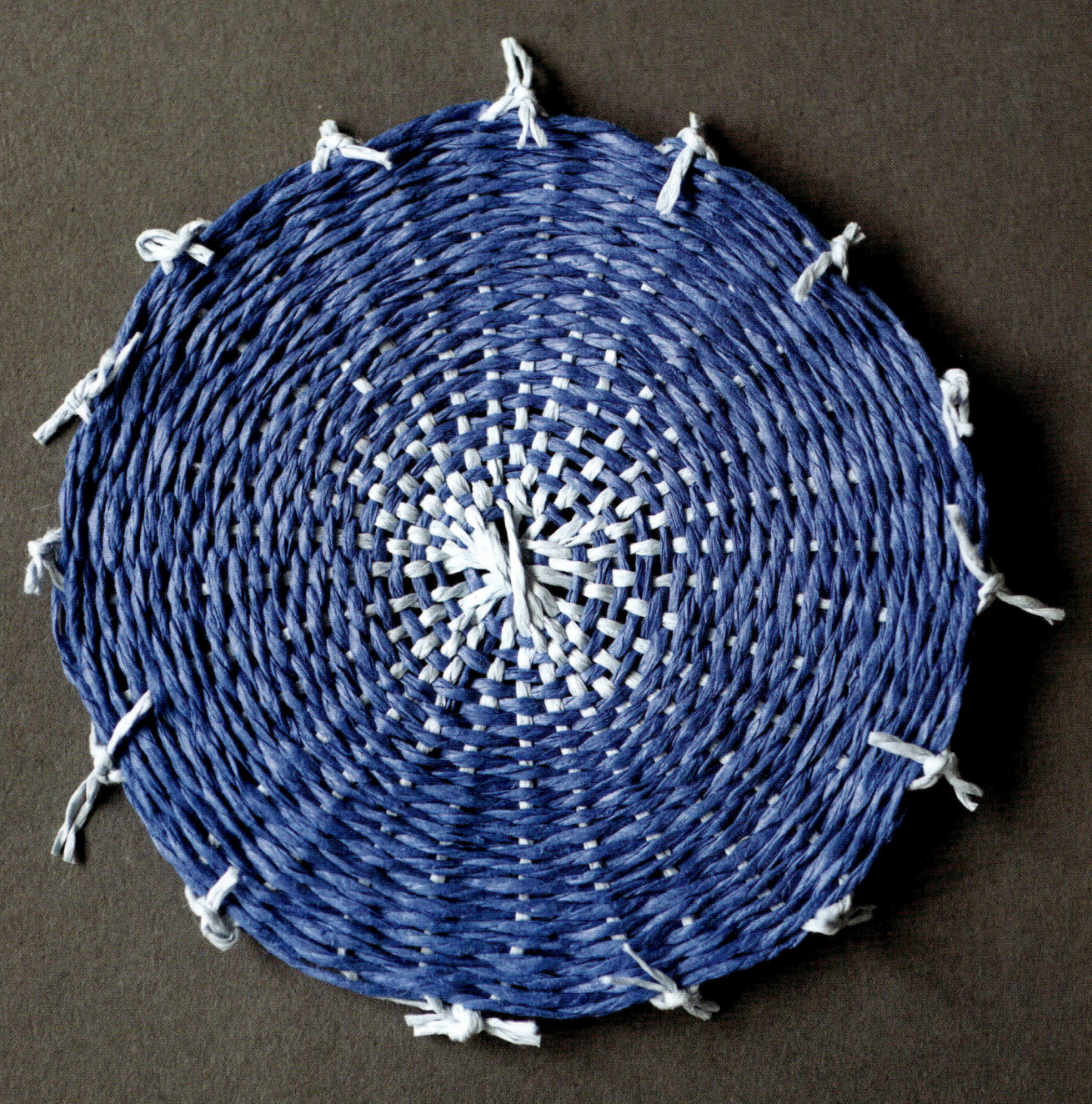

Woven Coasters by Andra Stanton.
Photo courtesy of Nate Castner.

Woven Coasters

BY ANDRA STANTON | ANDRASTANTON.COM

Skill Level: Beginner

SUPPLIES

- 2 colors of strong paper twine, 2,000 yards each (I purchased mine from paperphine.com) or homemade *kami-ito* (from 24" × 36" sheet of washi)

- 1 round kumihimo disk, 6-inch diameter, ⅜-inch dense foam (mine is The Beadsmith brand)

- 2 sheets of colored felt, 8.5" × 11", to match or coordinate with the yarn/twine

- 1 can of spray paint or jar of paint-on or spray-on matte or glossy varnish (I used Liquitex Professional Spray Varnish) (*optional*)

- 1 paintbrush (if using paint-on varnish) (*optional*)

- 1 large-eye blunt darning needle

- small container of hydrated methylcellulose glue powder (take care to follow manufacturer's directions)

- 1 small paint brush for applying methylcellulose

- 1 pencil

INSTRUCTIONS

1. Assign a number to each of your colors. Push Color 1 up through the open hole in the center of the disk, leaving a 5-inch tail. Hold the tail at the back of the disk and wedge the twine in the slot between 2 and 3. The twine will be at the back of the disk. Pull the twine from the back of the disk and wedge it into the slot between 3 and 4; the twine should now be at the front of the disk. Bring the twine across the front of the disk and wedge it into the opposite slot on the disk—in this case, in the slot between 18 and 19. The twine will be at the back of the disk. Pull the twine from the back of the disk and wedge it into the slot between 4 and 5; the twine should now be at the front of the disk. Bring the twine across the front of the disk and wedge it into the opposite slot on the disk—in this case, in the slot between 19 and 20.

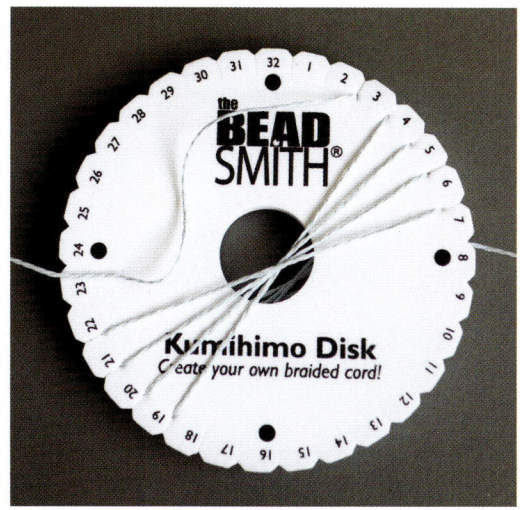

Step 1: Beginning to weave the coaster. *Note*: In this photo, the beginning tail has not been inserted in the hole in the disk. *Step photos courtesy of Nate Castner.*

2 Continue wedging and wrapping in this manner until all slots are filled *except* for the very last slot. Your twine will be at the back of the disk. Tie the end of the twine loosely to the beginning of the twine.

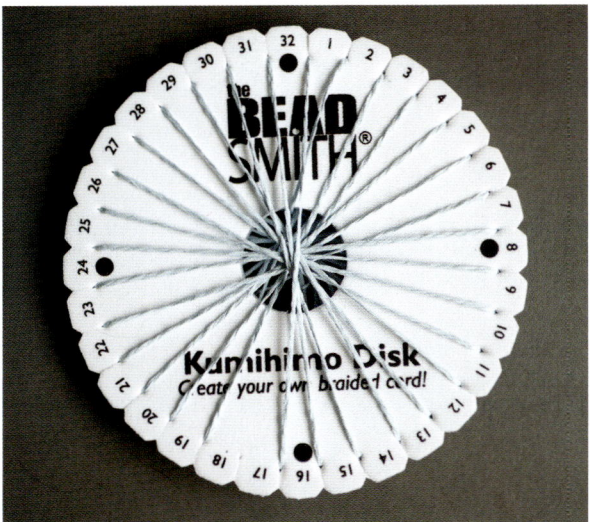

Step 2: Completed base of Color 1; the end is tied to the back of the disk.

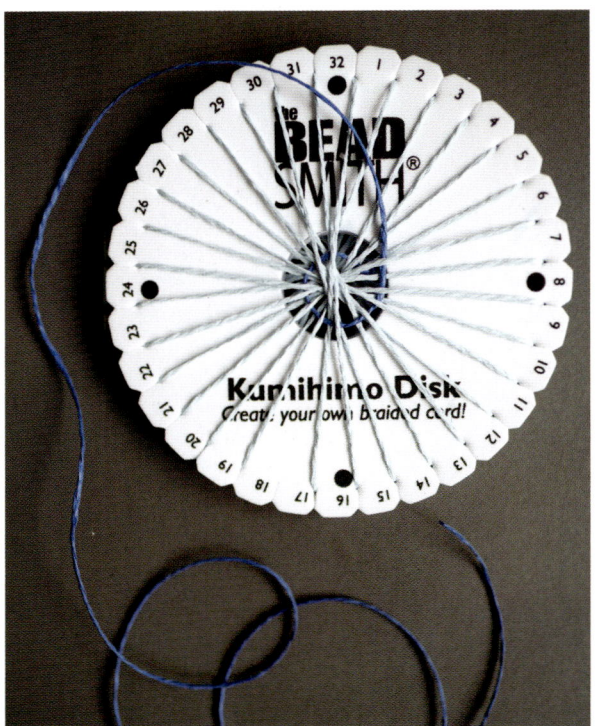

Step 5: Beginning to weave the Color 2 twine.

3 Measure 10 yards of the second color of yarn or twine and thread one end through the needle's eye.

4 Pull almost the entire length of Color 2 up through the open hole; leave a 5-inch tail as in Step 1.

5 Weave through the Color 1 twine by passing the needle under one stretched thread then over the next. Pull gently on the twine to tighten it when you are halfway around the circle.

6 Continue to weave the Color 2 twine over and under each succeeding piece of Color 1 twine until your coaster is the size you'd like it to be. Leaving a 5-inch tail, cut off Color 2 and tie it to the back of the piece. *Note:* To avoid tangles, I find it easiest to work standing up. Lay the disk in front of you on a table cleared of all other objects and keep the 10 yards of twine to one side. My right hand is my dominant hand, so I keep the pile of twine to the left side of my work.

7 Turn over the disk and make one big cut through all the Color 1 twine over the center of the hole. Pull the coaster from the disk.

8 Turn your coaster to the right side. The cut pieces of twine will be sticking out from the edge of the coaster. Double-knot every two adjacent threads together except for the last three. Knot those three pieces together. Snip the ends so that only ¼ inch of twine remains.

9 Weave the loose ends into the back of the coaster, taking care that none of them can be seen from the front. (You will be covering the back of the coaster with felt, so don't worry if it looks messy.)

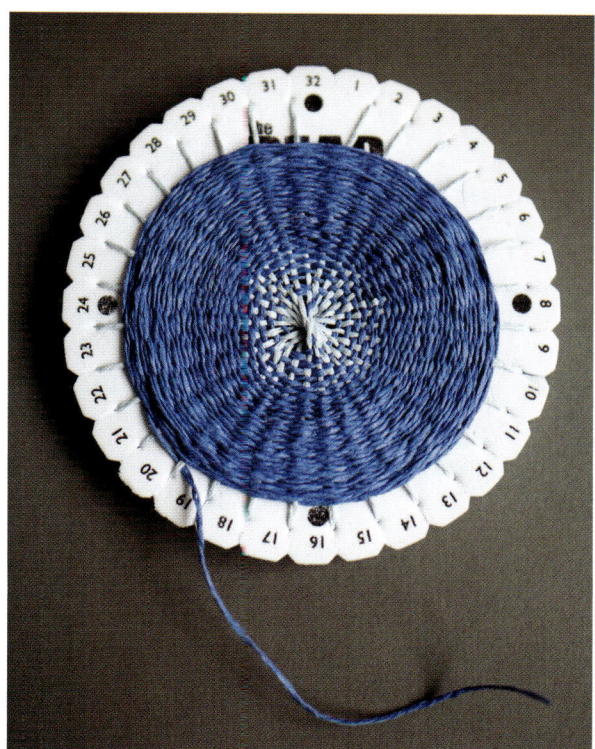

Step 6: Coaster woven to desired size.

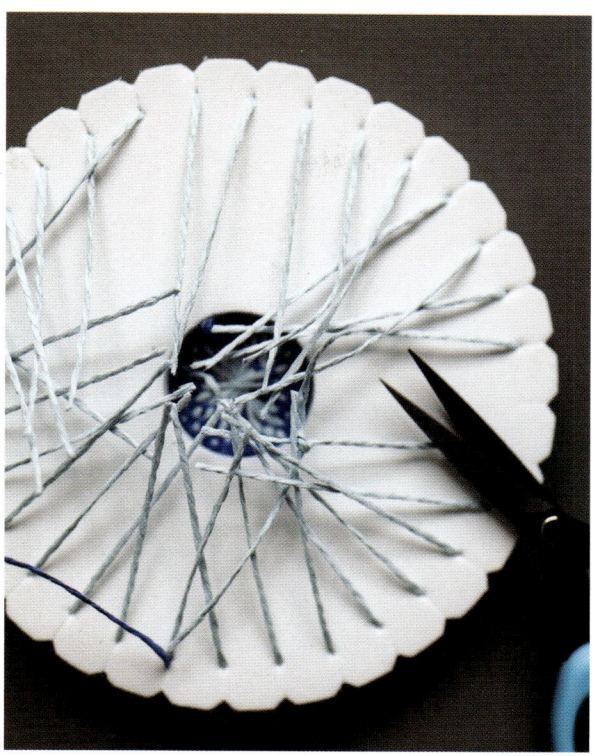

Step 7: Cutting through all the twine at the center back of the disk.

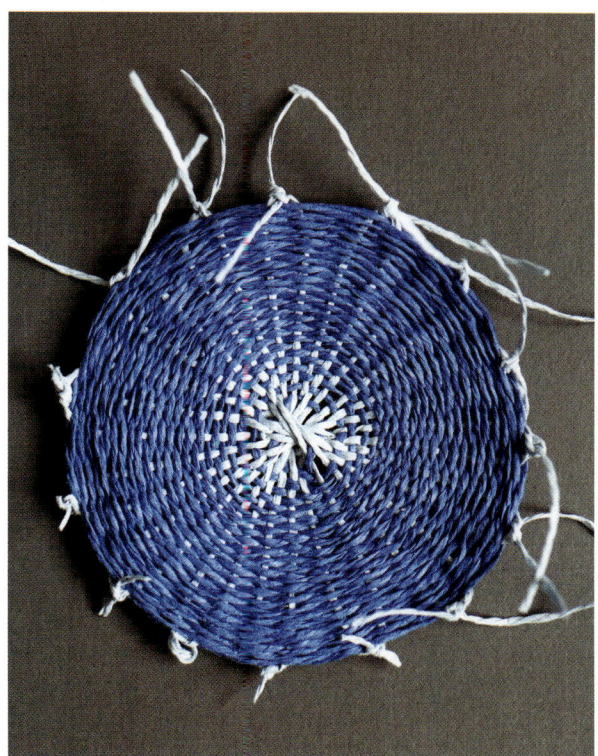

Step 8: Double-knotting adjacent threads at the edges of the front of the coaster.

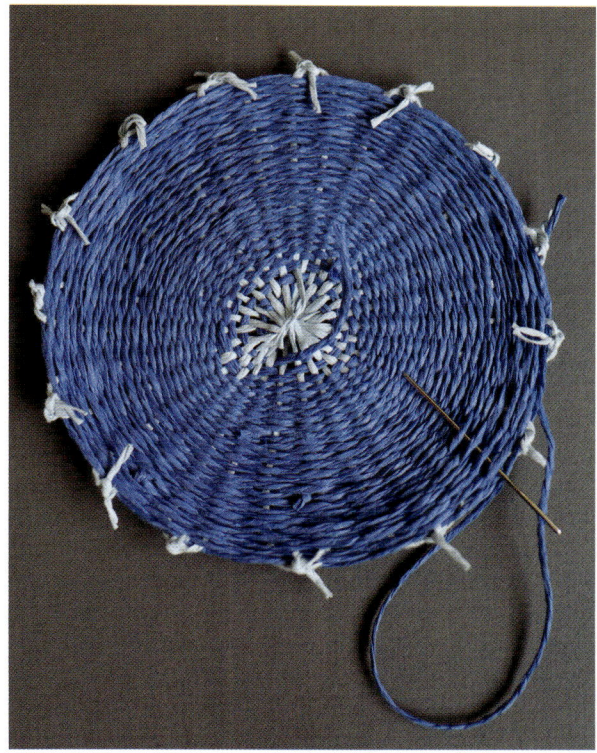

Step 9: Weaving the loose ends into the back of the coaster.

10 Spray the back of the coaster with varnish (or, using a small paint brush, apply paint-on varnish). Let dry. Then, spray (or paint) the front of the coaster with varnish and let dry.

11 With a pencil, trace the circumference of the coaster onto the felt sheet. Cut the circle a tiny bit smaller than the coaster, because you don't want the felt to show. Apply the methylcellulose to one side of the felt and press it firmly against the back of the coaster until it adheres.

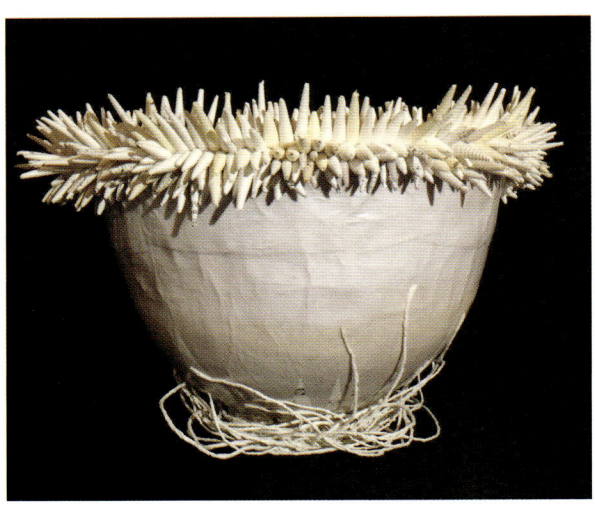

Flavia Lovatelli. *Ripple Effect*, 2017. 14" × 14" × 8.5". Paper coils, paper yarn. Assemblage. *Photo courtesy of Flavia Lovatelli. www.flavia-lovatelli.com*

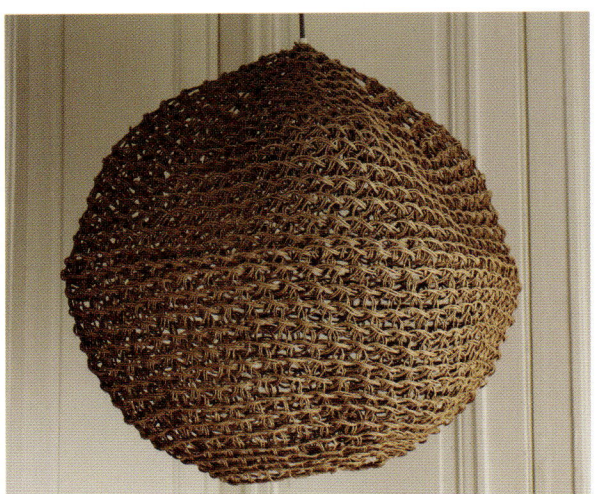

Kim Soon Ja. *Filet Double L Lampshade*, 2009. 27.5" (diameter). One hundred percent recycled paper. Macrame. *Photo courtesy of Corinne Muller & Piotr Oleszkowicz (Best Before). www.bestbefore.fr*

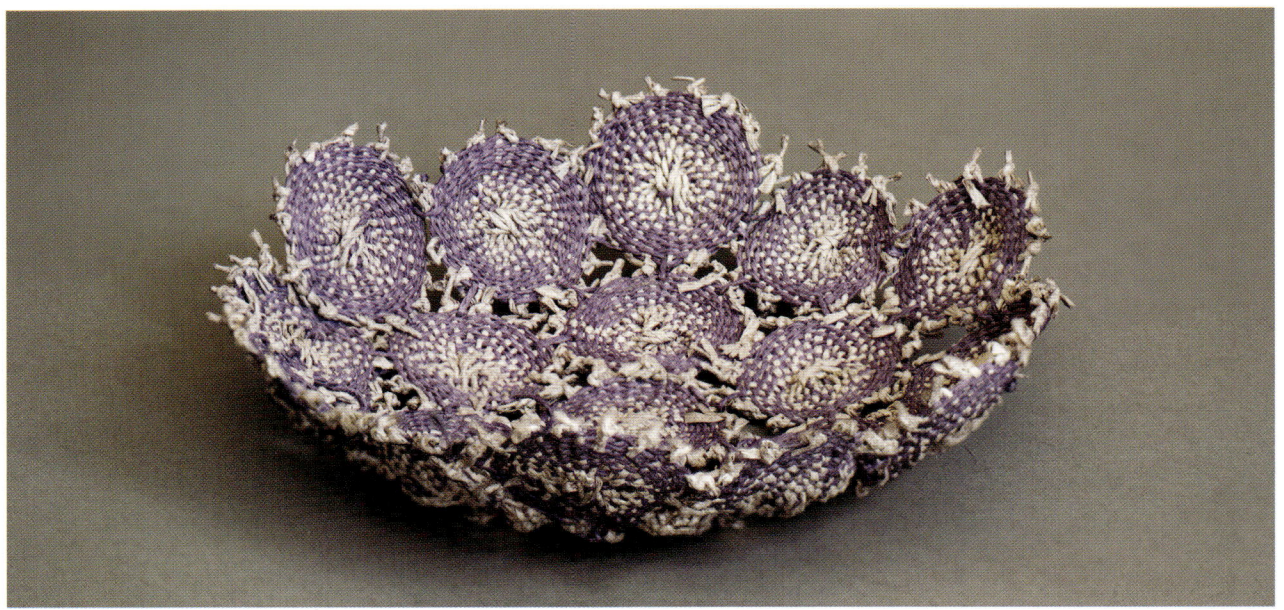

Andra Stanton. *Woven Paper Basket*, 2022. 12" × 2.5". Paper twine. Handwoven. *Photo courtesy of Nate Castner.* www.andrastanton.com

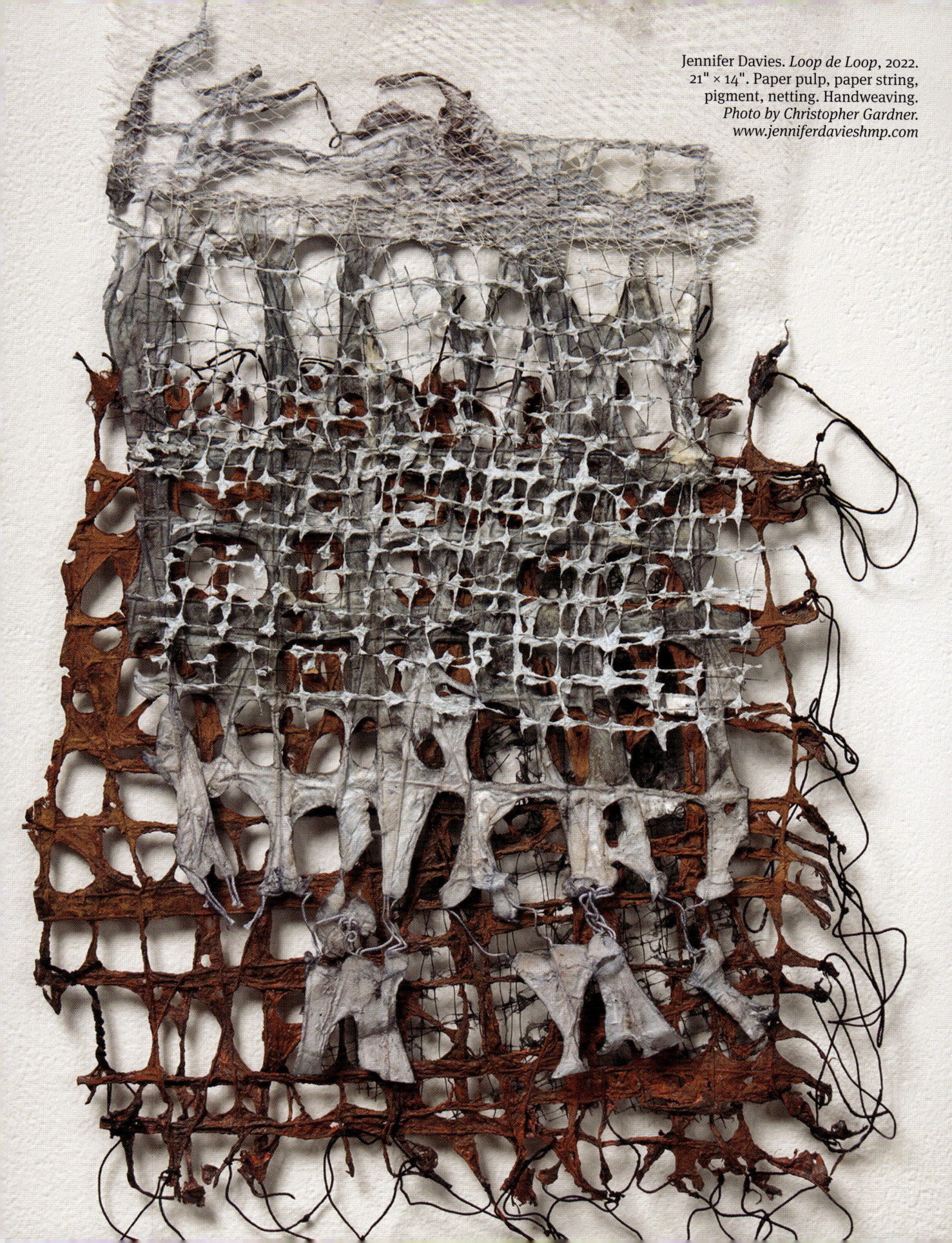

Jennifer Davies. *Loop de Loop*, 2022.
21" × 14". Paper pulp, paper string,
pigment, netting. Handweaving.
Photo by Christopher Gardner.
www.jenniferdavieshmp.com

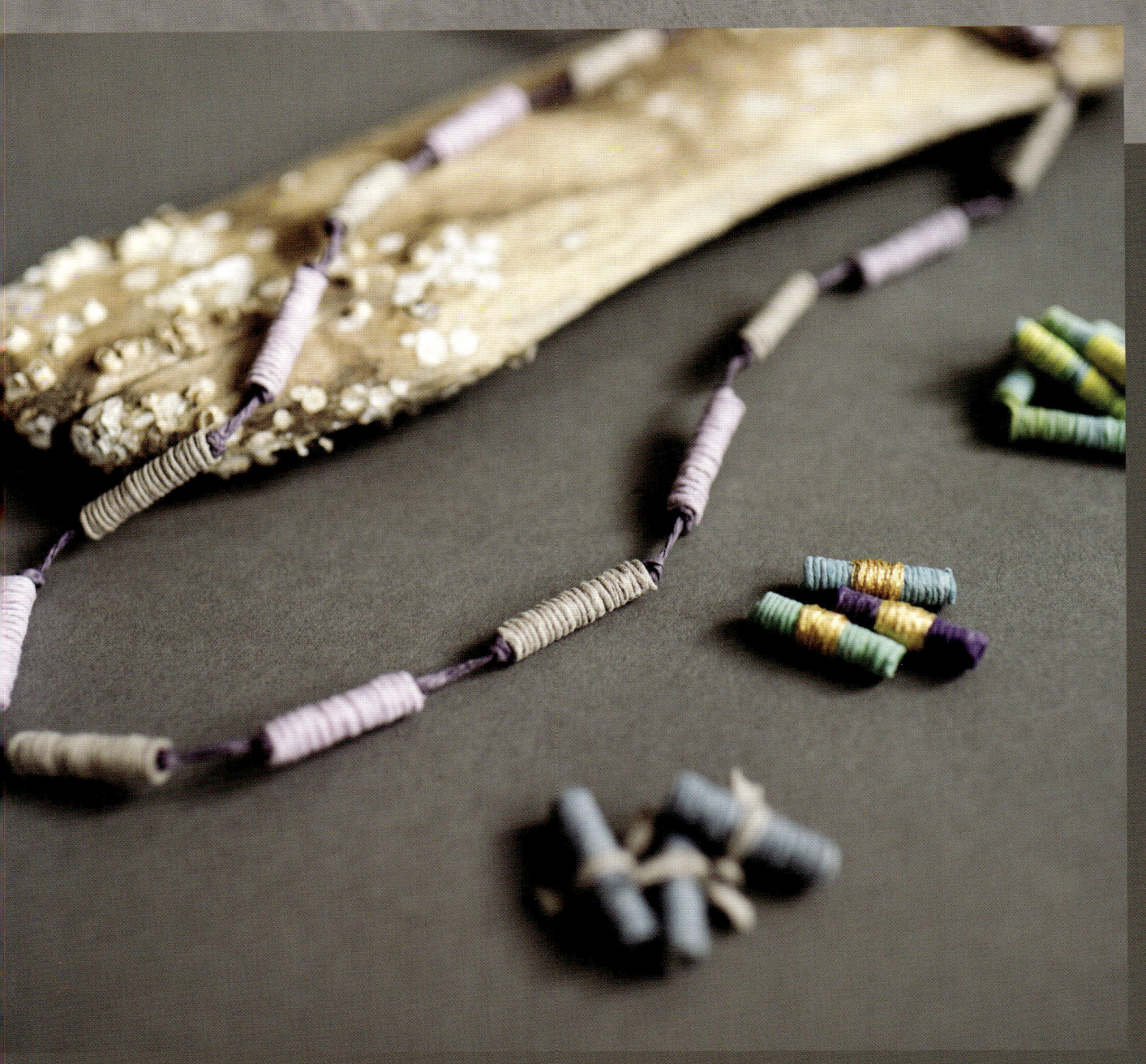

Paper Beads No. 1 by Andra Stanton.
Photo courtesy of Nate Castner.

Paper Beads No. 1

BY ANDRA STANTON | ANDRASTANTON.COM

Skill Level: Beginner

SUPPLIES

- 1 sheet kozo or other mulberry paper, 12" ×18", any color (I used Nara Natural Dyed Papers 25.5 g/m² in Indigo, Akebi Grey, and Sakaki Lilac from hiromipaper.com)

- 2 sheets of kraft paper, 8.5" ×11", *or* white or black construction paper

- 1 wooden skewer, metal knitting needle, or pencil

- small container of hydrated methylcellulose glue powder (take care to follow manufacturer's directions)

- 1 small paint brush for applying methylcellulose

- 1 bottle tie-dye spray paint or any liquid acrylic or watercolor paint (if not using predyed papers) (*optional*)

- twine for stringing paper beads

- matte or glossy varnish (I used Liquitex Professional Spray Varnish) (*optional*)

- 1 pair 3 mm crimp clasps with crimping tool or flat-nose pliers (*optional*)

INSTRUCTIONS

1. If using spray paint, fluid acrylics, or watercolors, paint the neutral washi in the colors you prefer to use to make your paper beads. Let dry.

2. Cut the washi into ¼-inch strips.

3. Spray the strips with water until they are slightly damp.

4. Twist all the strips of paper tightly between your forefinger and thumb until you have made thread. If small areas begin to unfold, tighten your twists. If the paper strips *still* won't cooperate, apply diluted methylcellulose to your thumb and index finger and twist again. Let dry.

5. Cut the kraft or construction paper into a 1-inch by 1-inch piece and wrap one piece around the skewer.

6. Secure the loose end of the construction paper to the rolled construction paper with a dab of methylcellulose.

7 With a brush, apply a thin coat of methylcellulose to one end of the construction paper tube. Adhere the start of the thread to the construction tube. Hold the thread in place until it dries.

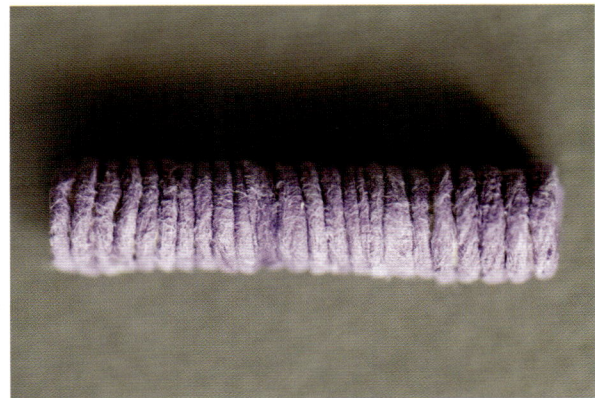

Step 9: A finished paper bead.

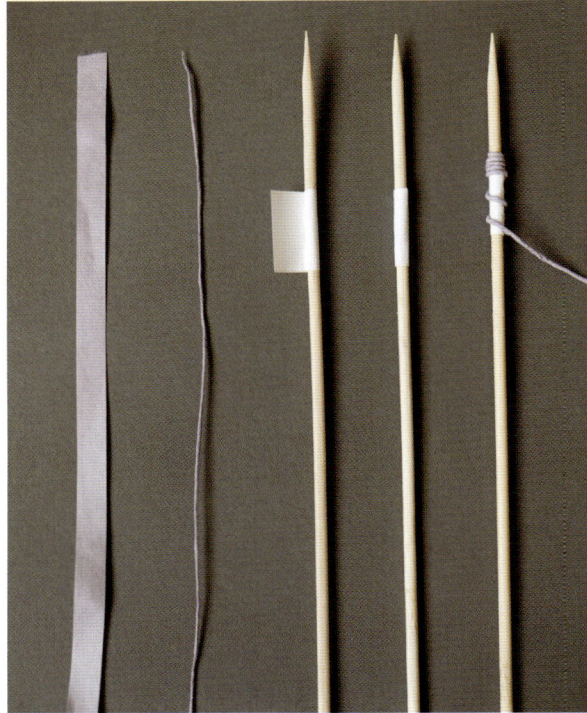

Steps 2 through 7: Progression of instructions using paper and dowel. *Step photos courtesy of Nate Castner.*

8 Add methylcellulose to more of the tube and continue to wrap the thread tightly around the base paper, making sure each piece of thread abuts the one next to it. If needed, apply a little bit of methylcellulose to the tube as you continue to wrap the thread. Finish wrapping at the end of the base paper and cut off the extra thread. Let dry.

9 Remove the finished paper bead from the skewer. You can leave the beads as they are, or paint or spray them with the matte or gloss varnish to seal them.

10 Repeat Steps 5 through 9 until you have made as many beads as you'd like for your necklace.

11 String the beads onto the twine. Secure each bead in place by making a double knot before and after each bead. I applied some methylcellulose onto each knot with the tip of a skewer to keep them secure.

12 Finish the necklace by tying a knot or using a crimp clasp. Squeeze crimps several times with a crimp tool or flat-nose pliers.

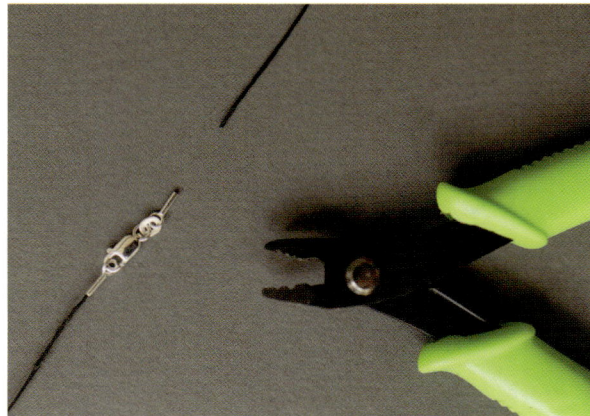

Step 12: Using crimp clasp and crimp tool.

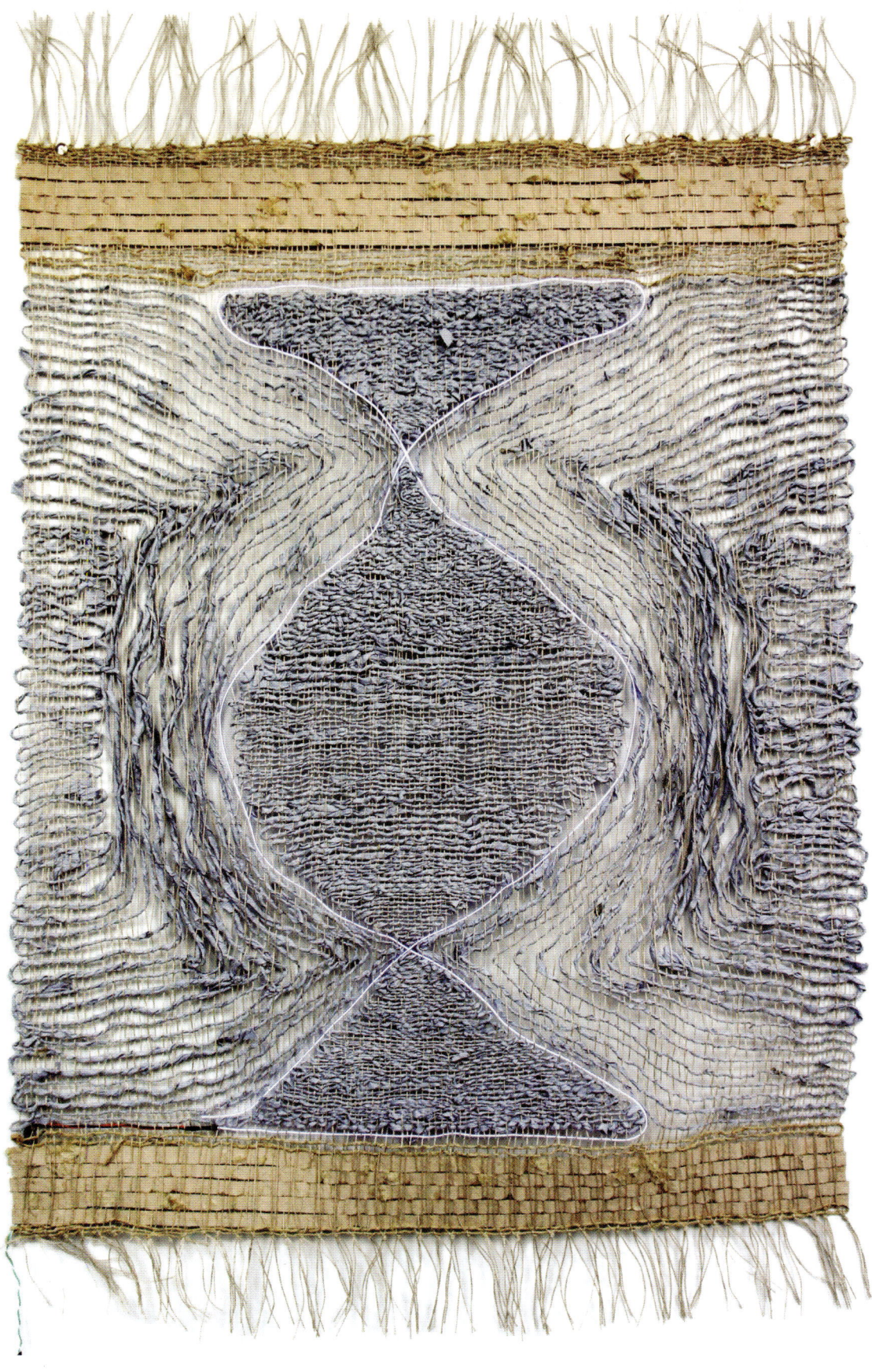

Melissa Hilliard Potter. *Tusheti Rug*, 2022. 40" × 60". Handspun, handmade quilt scraps; paper; okra paper; wire. Tapestry loom woven, drop-spindled paper thread. *Photo courtesy of Melissa Hilliard Potter. www.melpotter.com*

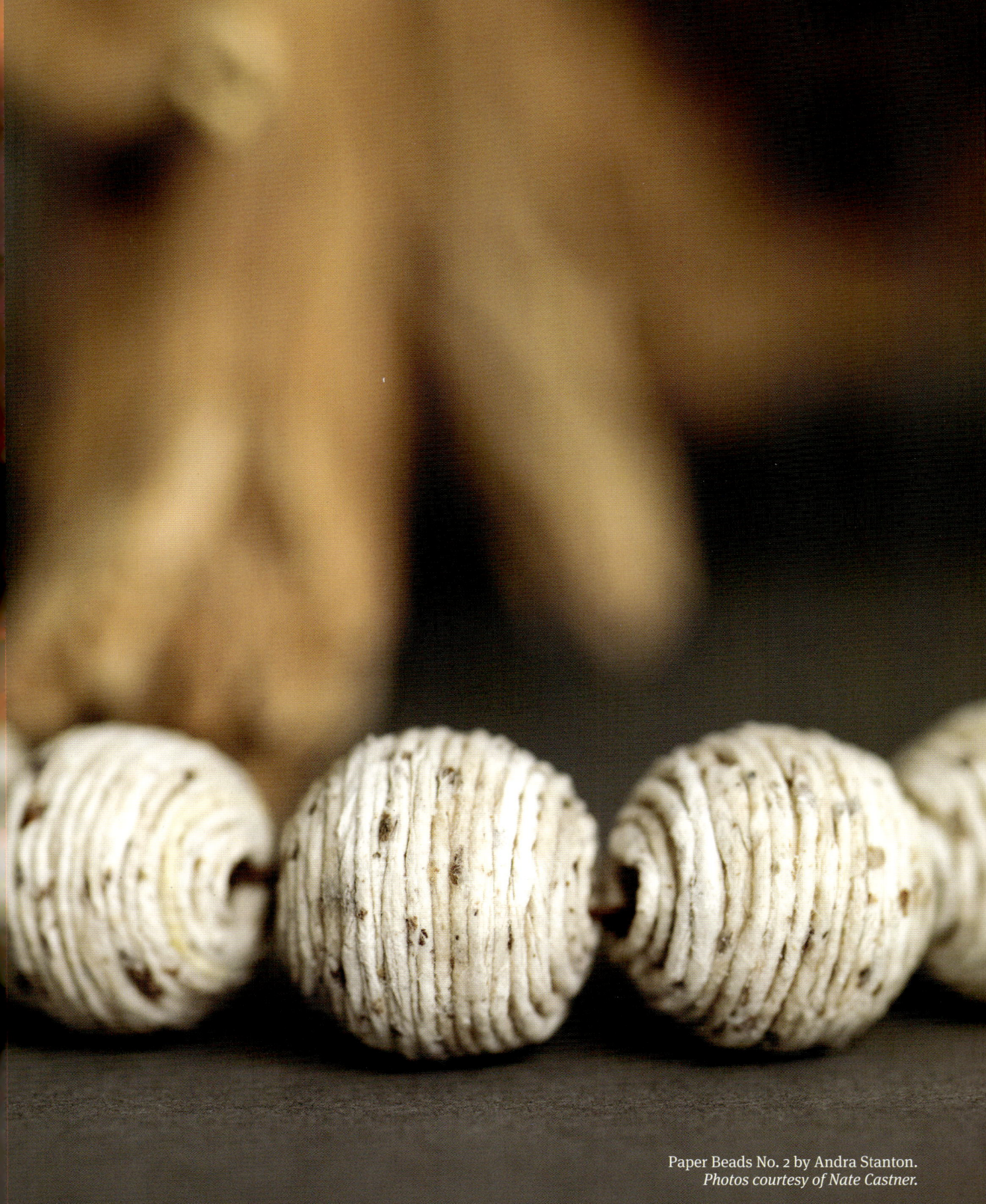

Paper Beads No. 2 by Andra Stanton.
Photos courtesy of Nate Castner.

Paper Beads No. 2

BY ANDRA STANTON | ANDRASTANTON.COM

Skill Level: Beginner

SUPPLIES

- kozo or other mulberry paper, 12" × 18" sheet
- 1 fine-mist spray bottle
- 16-mm wood beads

- small container of hydrated methylcellulose glue powder (take care to follow manufacturer's directions)
- 1 small paint brush for applying methylcellulose

- waxed linen (I used 4-ply)
- 1 pair 3 mm crimp clasps with crimping tool or flat-nose pliers (*optional*)

INSTRUCTIONS

1. Cut the mulberry paper into ¼-inch strips.

2. Spray one strip lightly with water until it's slightly damp.

3. Twist the paper tightly between your forefinger and thumb until you have made thread. If small areas begin to unfold, tighten your twists. If the paper strips *still* won't cooperate, apply diluted methylcellulose to your thumb and index finger, and twist again. Let dry.

4. Repeat Steps 2 and 3 until you have multiple pieces of yarn. Connect them by gluing and twisting them together at their ends.

5. Take 1 bead and apply a tiny bit of glue near one of the bead holes.

6. Anchor one end of the yarn in the glue and hold for several seconds, until it adheres.

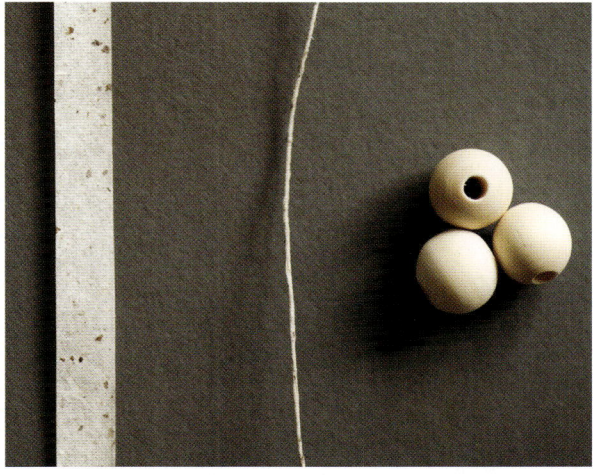

Step 3: A strip of washi, a finished piece of thread, and the beads around which to wrap it.

7 Using the small brush, paint a thin layer of glue onto the wooden bead, then wrap the yarn around it, and let it dry.

8 Repeat Steps 5 through 7 to make as many beads as you desire for your necklace.

9 String the beads onto a length of waxed linen that is long enough for your necklace.

10 Feed each end of the waxed linen into a crimp clasp and squeeze the crimp tightly using the crimping tool or pliers. Squeeze the crimp several times along its length.

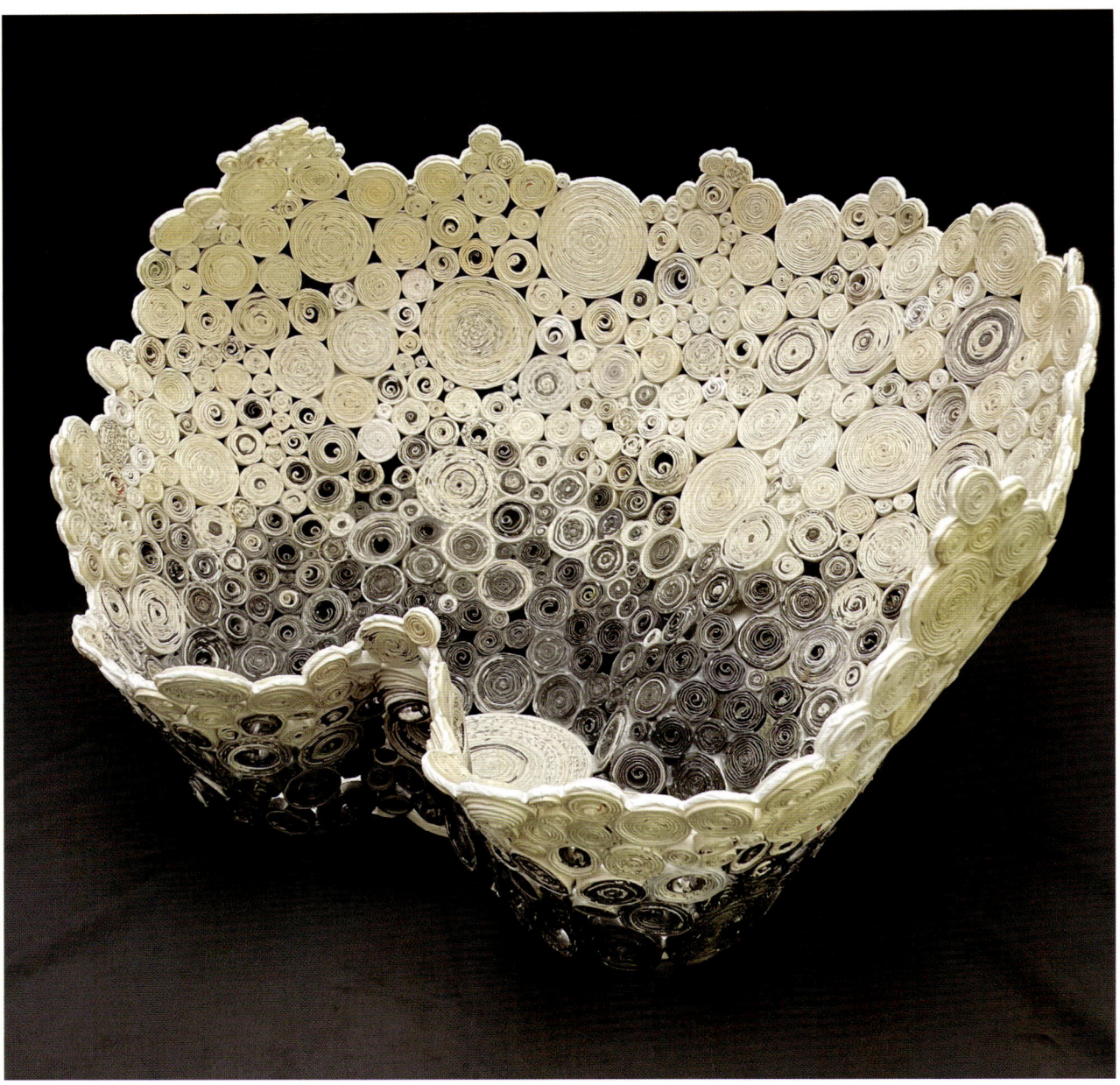

Flavia Lovatelli. *Black and White*, 2021. 13" × 19" × 15". Recycled magazines. Paper coilings, assemblage. *Photo courtesy of Flavia Lovatelli. www.flavia-lovatelli.com*

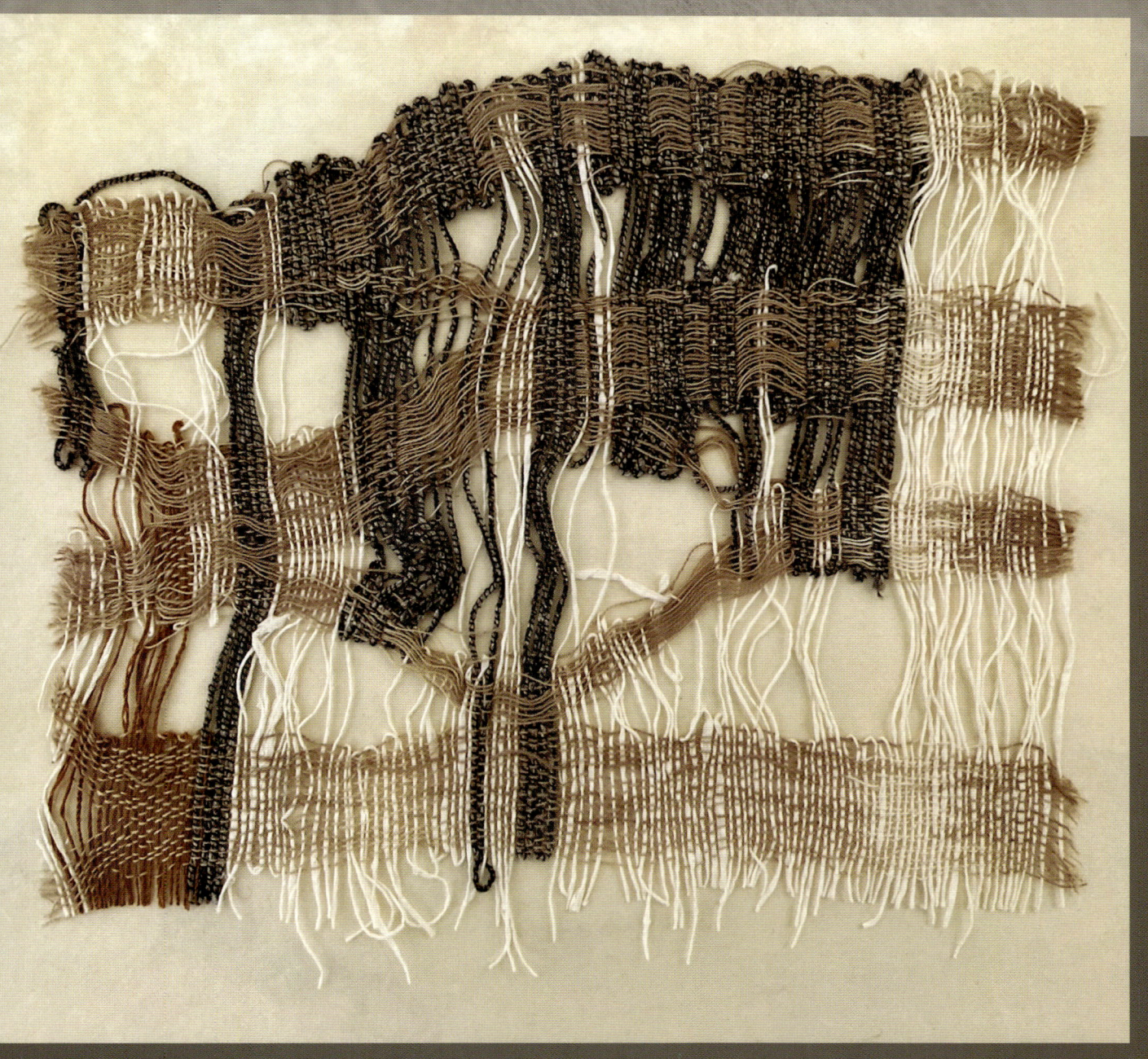

Suzi Ballenger. *Fragment Migration*, 2017. 8.5" × 10.5".
Handspun kozo (single ply), linden bark (hands-on,
in Japan), wrapped silk thread. Hand-dyed cotton
warp with sandalwood pigment. Handwoven. *Photo
courtesy of Suzi Ballenger. www.realfibers.com*

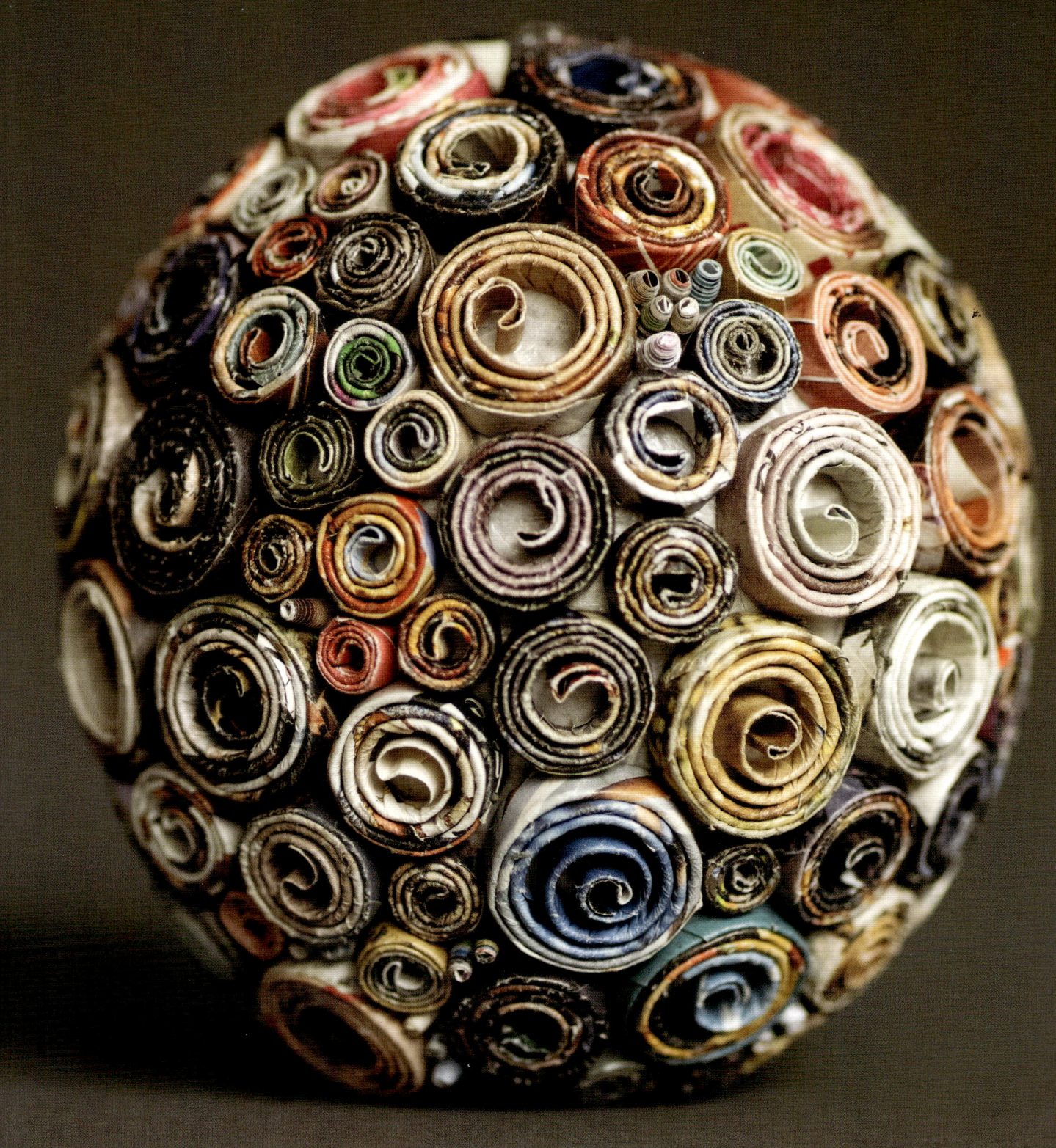

Paper Spores Globe by Flavia Lovatelli.
Photo courtesy of Nate Castner.

Paper Spores Globe

BY FLAVIA LOVATELLI | FLAVIA-LOVATELLI.COM

Skill Level: Beginner

This project uses paper strips rather than paper yarn, but it's worth enjoying this artist's work and experimenting with how different formats of paper can contribute to your creations.

SUPPLIES

- 1 colorful magazine

- 1 paper cutter or pair of scissors

- white PVA glue

- 1 small, shallow container

- 1 coiling tool (I used the Floranea slotted paper quilling tool)

- 1 wooden skewer

- 1 scrapbooking scoring tool *or* the back of a butterknife

- 1 small craft brush

- 1 clear plastic globe (I used a 4" size) *or* a homemade paper mâché globe (see additional instructions)

INSTRUCTIONS

1 Using a paper cutter or scissors, cut the pages from the magazine—as close to the spine as possible—making sure you have crisp, straight edges.

2 Again using the paper cutter, slice all the pages in half vertically. Cut some of them in half and in quarters to create a variety of sizes.

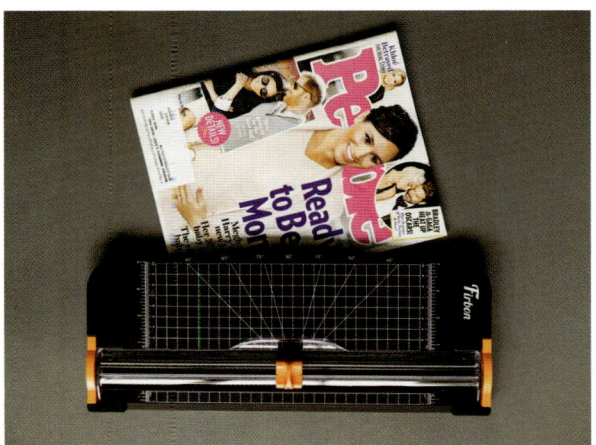

Step 1: Preparing to cut pages from a colorful magazine using a paper cutter. *Step photos courtesy of Nate Castner.*

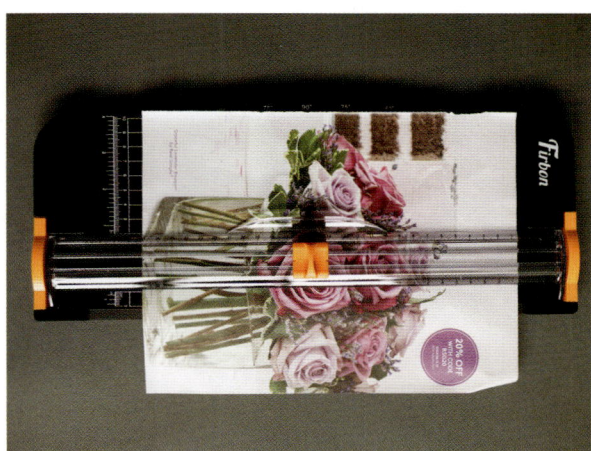

Step 2: Using the paper cutter to cut pages in half vertically.

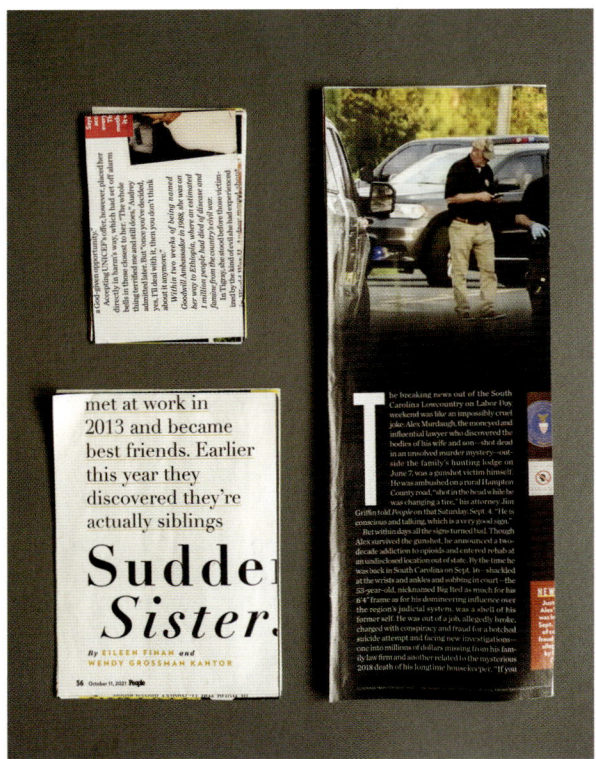

Step 2: Creating a variety of sizes.

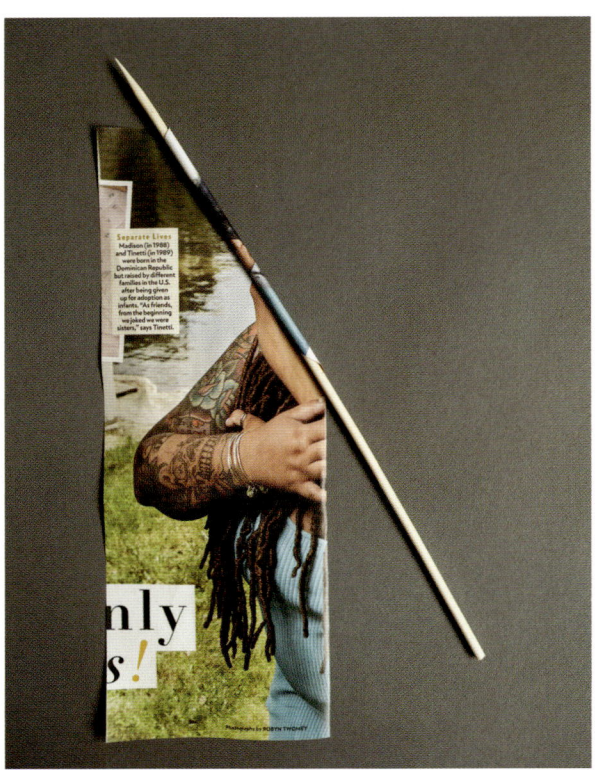

Step 4: Rolling the paper onto a skewer at a 45-degree angle.

3. Take a skewer and place it at the corner of the magazine strip at a 45-degree angle.

4. Roll the strip tightly, using the skewer.

5. Make sure the roll is even at both ends so that the rolled strip resembles a straw, not a cone.

6. Place a small dab of glue on the tip of your finger and adhere the loose corner to the rolled strip. The less glue you use, the faster the paper becomes fixed.

7. Remove the skewer from the paper.

8. Repeat Steps 3 through 7 until you have multiple rolls.

9. Flatten all rolls, one at a time, with the scoring tool or the handle of a butterknife.

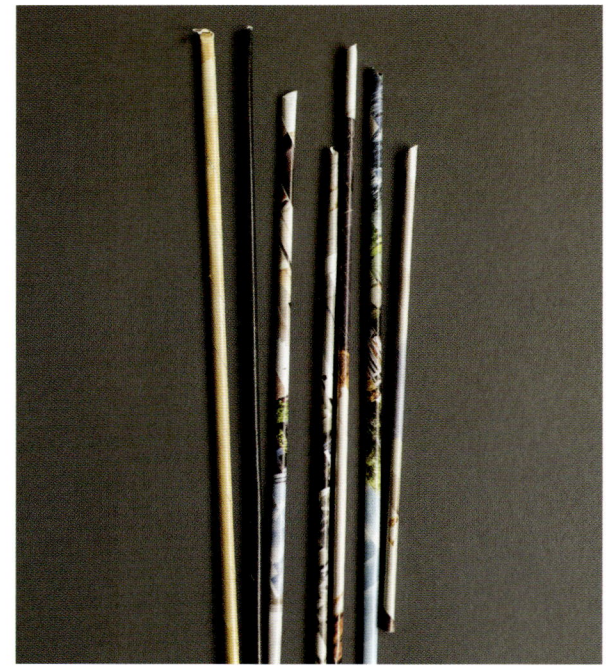

Step 8: Multiple rolls of paper.

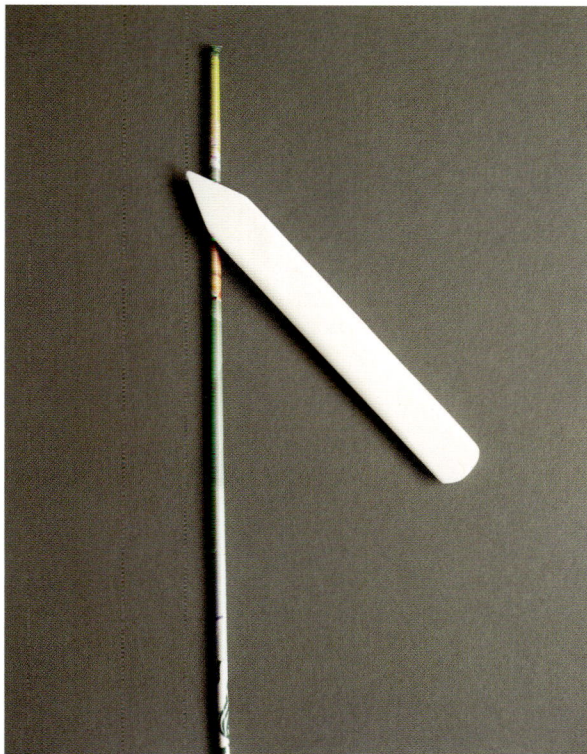

Step 9: Flattening a roll of paper.

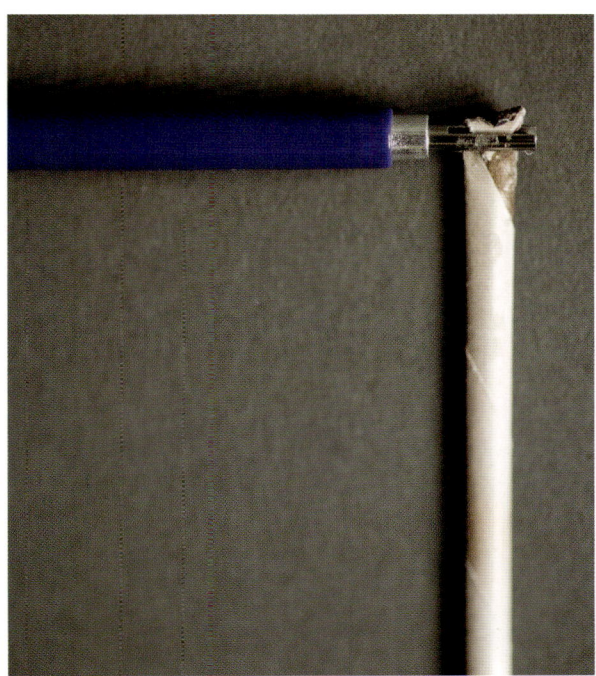

Step 10: Using the quilling tool to begin rolling the paper.

10 Use the coiling/quilling tool to coil the flattened strips. Insert one end of a flattened strip into the opening of the tool, twirl the tool, and roll the entire strip.

11 Remove the tool gently from the coil. Repeat Steps 10 and 11 until you have enough coils to cover your globe.

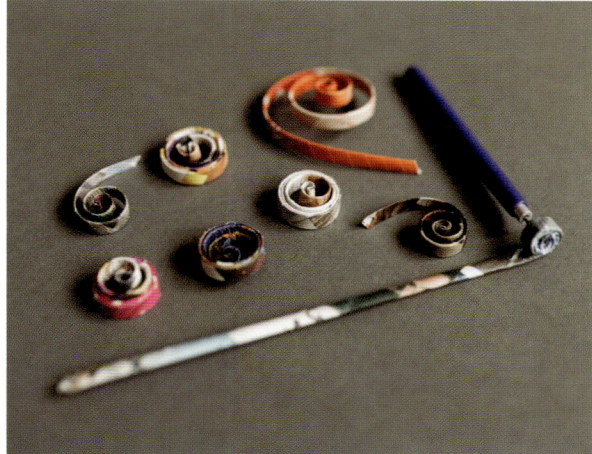

Step 11: Making multiple coils.

12 Tighten each coil by pulling on the end. Add a dab of glue to the end and press it against the tightened coil, holding it for a few seconds, until the coil, or quill, adheres to itself. Repeat for the rest of the quills.

13 Place approximately 2 tablespoons of glue into the small, shallow container.

14 Using the small brush, pick up some glue and apply it to the entire underside of a quill. Press the quill onto the globe, holding it for a few seconds until the quill adheres.

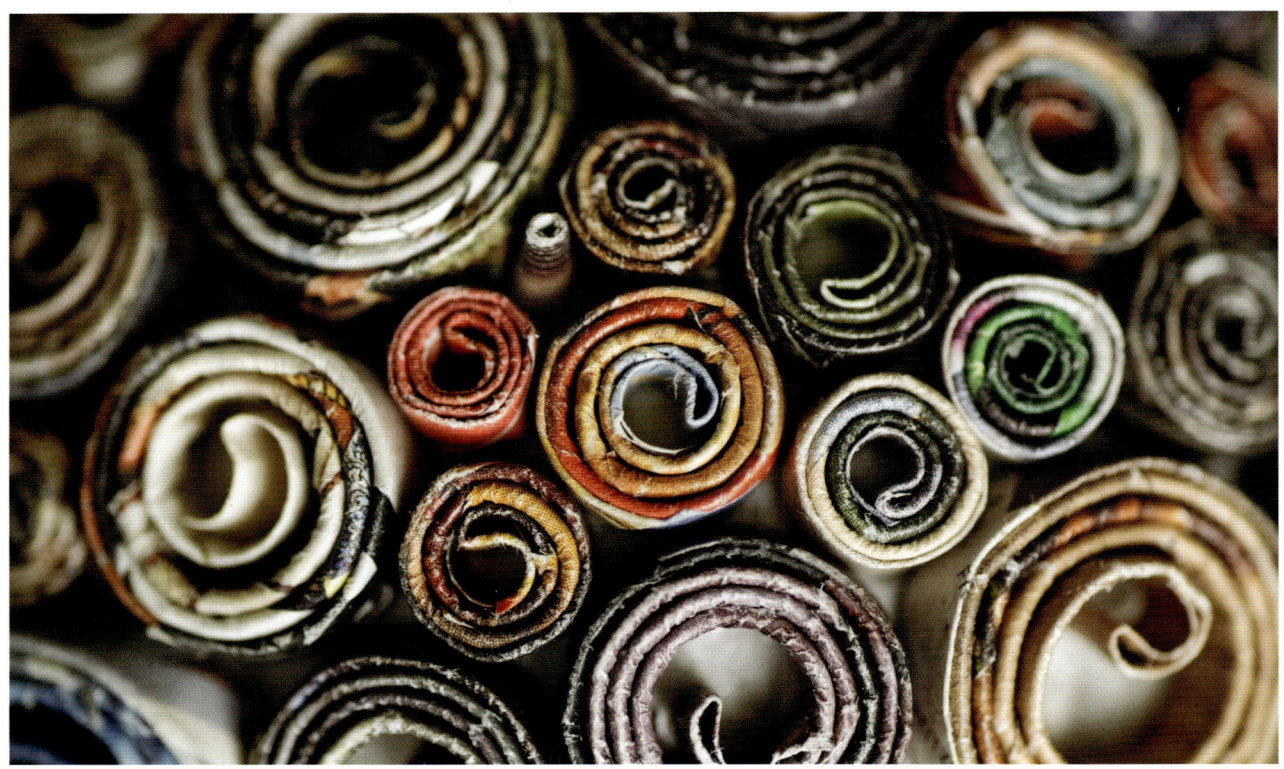

Step 14: Adhering quills to the globe.

15 Use the smaller quills to fill the "holes" on your globe.

HOW TO MAKE A PAPER MÂCHÉ GLOBE

SUPPLIES

- 8.5" × 11" strips of magazine-page paper, as many as needed to cover your globe
- 1 balloon
- 5 tbsp. boiling water
- 1 tbsp. all-purpose flour

- 1 pinch of salt
- 1 small bowl
- 1 wooden spoon
- 1 straight pin
- white PVA glue

INSTRUCTIONS

1 Blow up the balloon until it is the size you want for your globe.

2 Make the paper mâché by first boiling the water.

3 Pour the boiling water into a small bowl. Add the flour and salt. Stir until smooth. Let the mixture thicken and cool enough so that you can handle it without burning your hands. If the mixture is too thick, add a bit more water.

4 Dip the paper strips into the flour mixture. Remove any excess mixture by pulling the strips of paper between your fingers.

5 Cover the entire balloon with paper— about 7 layers—*except* for a space around the knot of the balloon.

6 When the globe is dry (about 24 hours), use the pin to pop the balloon and remove it through the hole.

7 Seal the hole with a couple of layers of paper using *glue* instead of the flour mixture.

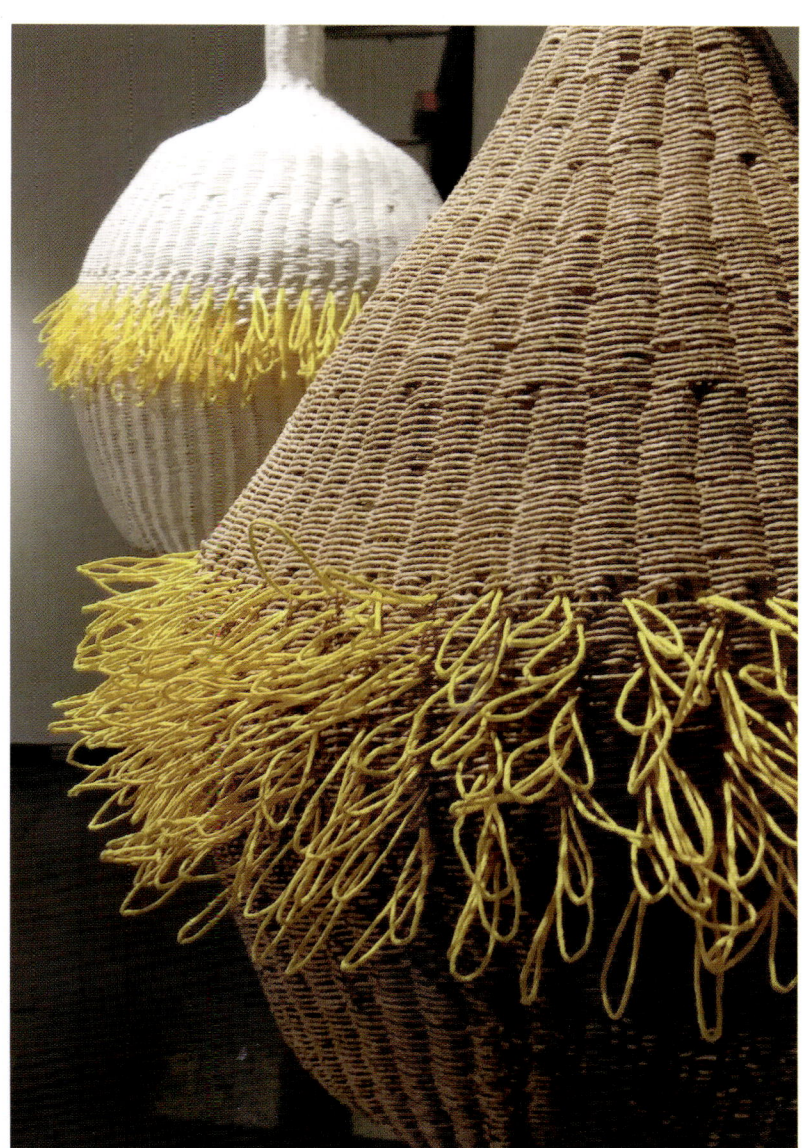

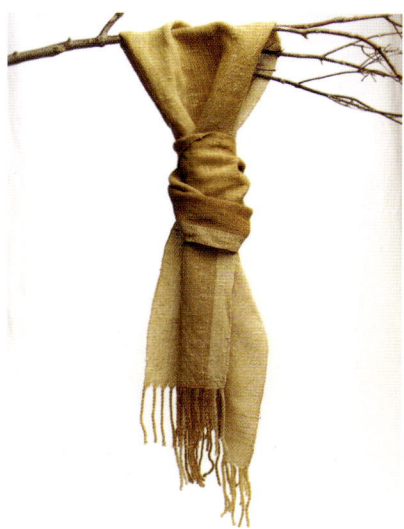

Above: Chiara Tizian, *Paper Scarf*, 2019. 70" × 14.5". Handspun Japanese paper yarn dyed with birch bark and pomegranate. Handwoven on wool warp with a rigid heddle loom. *Photo courtesy of Chiara Tizian.* *www.chiaratizian.com*

Marie-José Gustave. *Fruit*, 2018. 9.8" × 12.2". Installation of two suspended works (detail). Paper yarn. Basketry. *Photo courtesy of Marie-José Gustave.* *www.mariejosegustave.com*

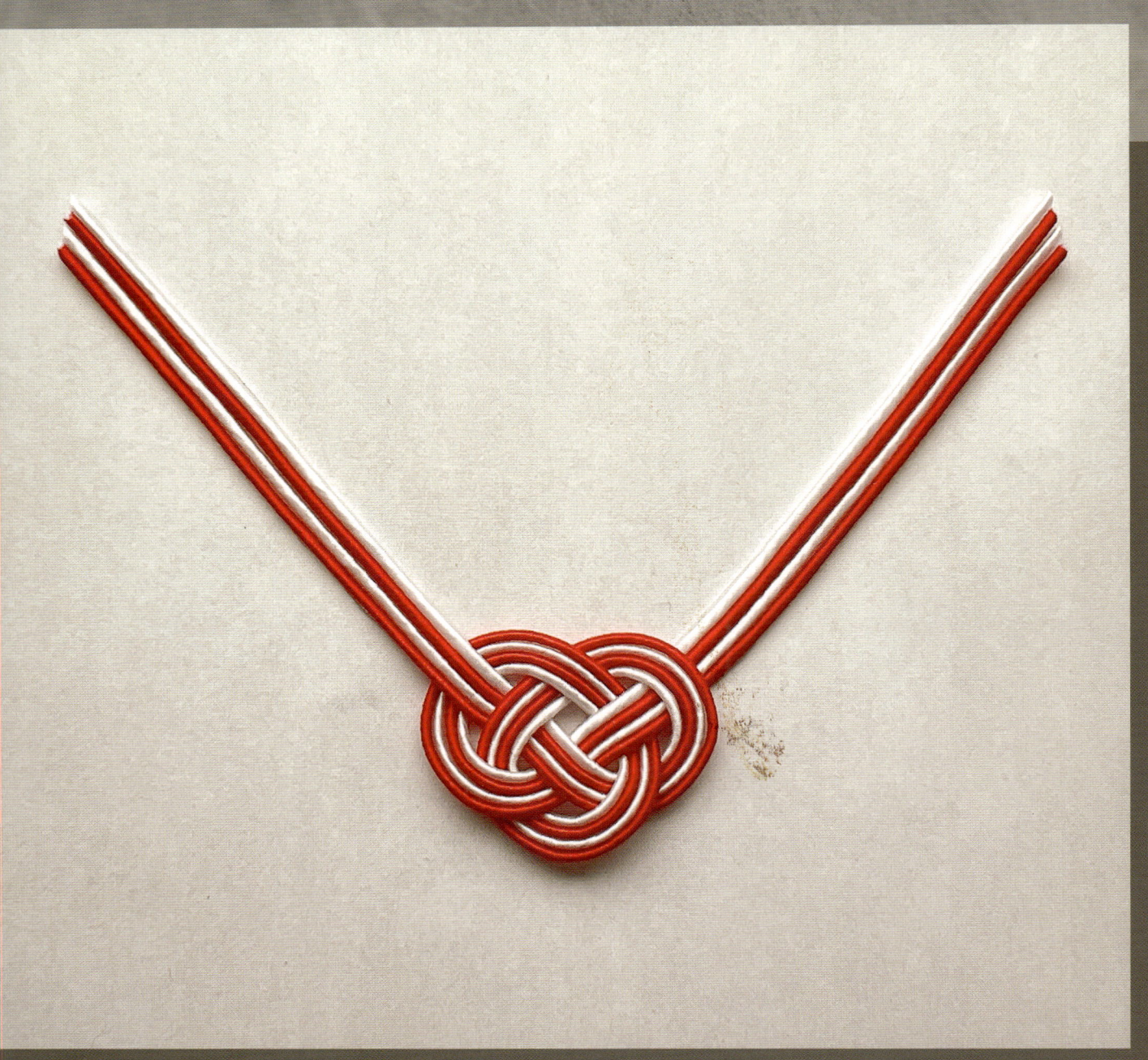

Mizuhiki Knot by Satoi Adams (Kobayashi)
Photo courtesy of Satoi Adams (Kobayashi).

Mizuhiki Knot, or Awaji Musubi

BY SATOI ADAMS (KOBAYASHI) | MIZUHIKIGLOBALLINKS.COM

Skill Level: Beginner

SUPPLIES

- red and white *mizuhiki* cords

INSTRUCTIONS

1 Cut three 24-inch pieces of cord—two in red and one in white. Bend the cords into a symmetric U shape and fold the left cords over the right cords to form a small teardrop shape.

2 Bend the left cords over the middle of the teardrop shape to form a pretzel shape.

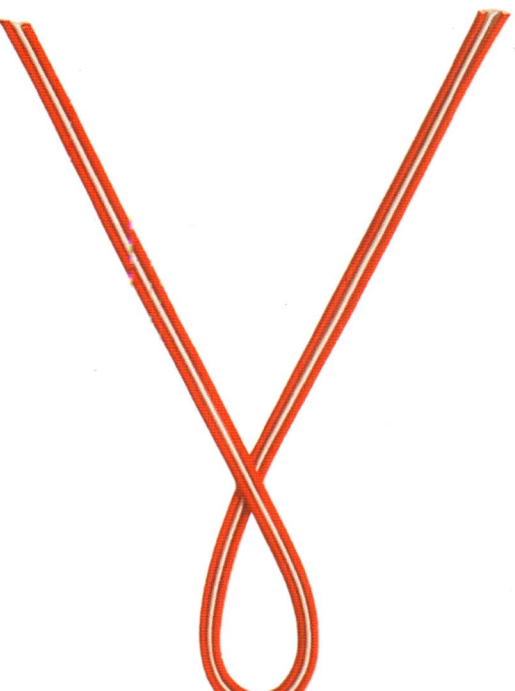

Step 1: Bending cords into a symmetric tear-drop shape. *Step photos courtesy of Satoi Adams (Kobayashi).*

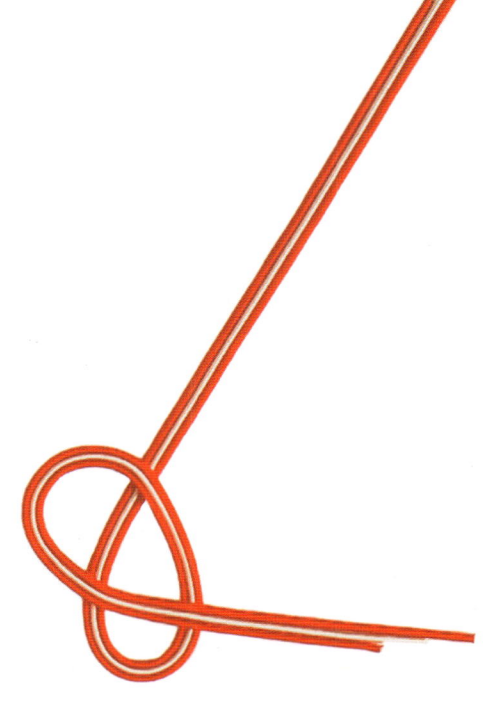

Step 2: Bending the left cords over the middle of the teardrop to form a pretzel shape.

3 Fold the top cords over the bottom ones and cut off any extra length from the top cord. The lengths of the two ends of the cording should be approximately the same.

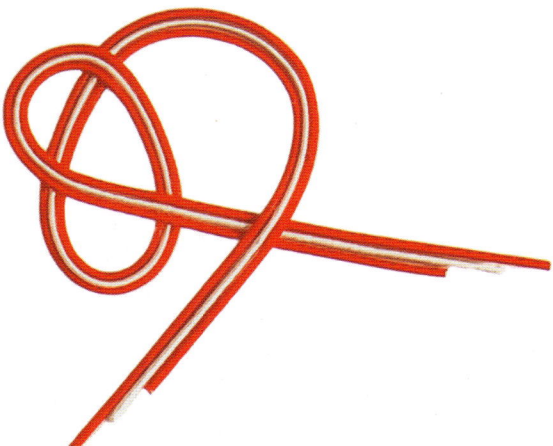

Step 3: Folding the top cords over the bottom ones and cutting off any extra length from the top cord.

4 Holding the cord you just cut, insert it through the back of the bottom hole of the pretzel shape.

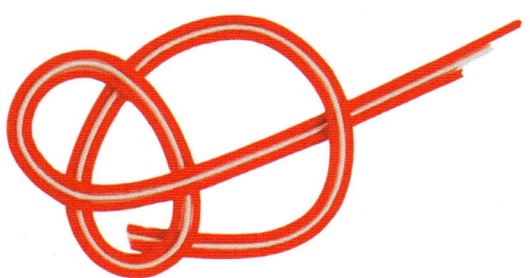

Step 4: Inserting the cord you just cut through the back of the bottom hole of the pretzel shape.

5 Still holding the same cord, pull it up over the cord directly above it and insert it through the middle hole of the pretzel shape, under the cord in front of it, and over the top edge the pretzel shape.

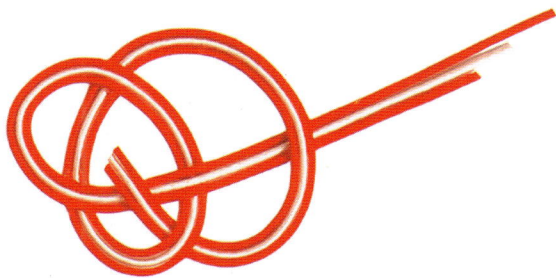

Step 5: Pulling the same cord up through the bottom pretzel hole and preparing to insert it through the middle pretzel hole.

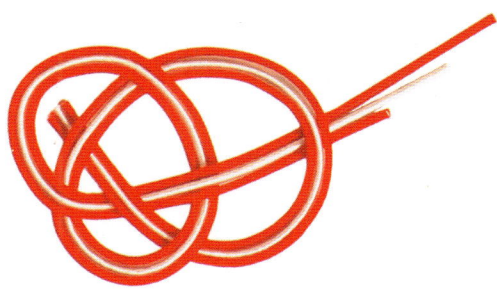

Step 5: Inserting the same cord down through the middle pretzel hole and up through the top pretzel hole. *Note:* The photo does not show the left cord laying over the top cord of the pretzel shape.

6 Pull the right piece of cording (the one you haven't been using) carefully, making sure the colors align in the pattern you want. Then, pull the other cord gently to create a symmetric *awaji musubi*.

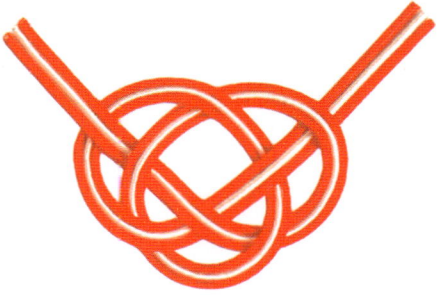

Step 6: Pulling the other cord gently to create the knot.

7 This step is optional. To minimize the teardrop shape at the center of the *awaji musubi*, pull the two upper ring parts apart gently. Then, pull *each cord*, one by one, in order, beginning with the inside cord. This results in a tighter *awaji musubi*.

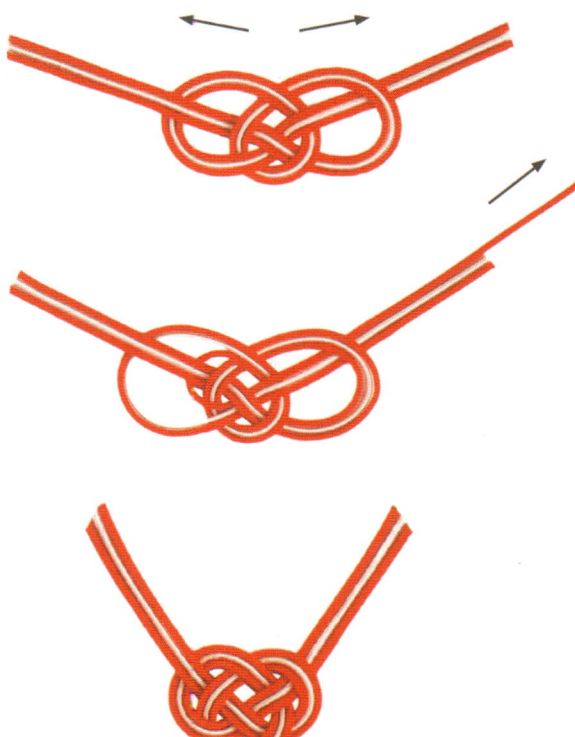

Step 7: Tightening the knot.

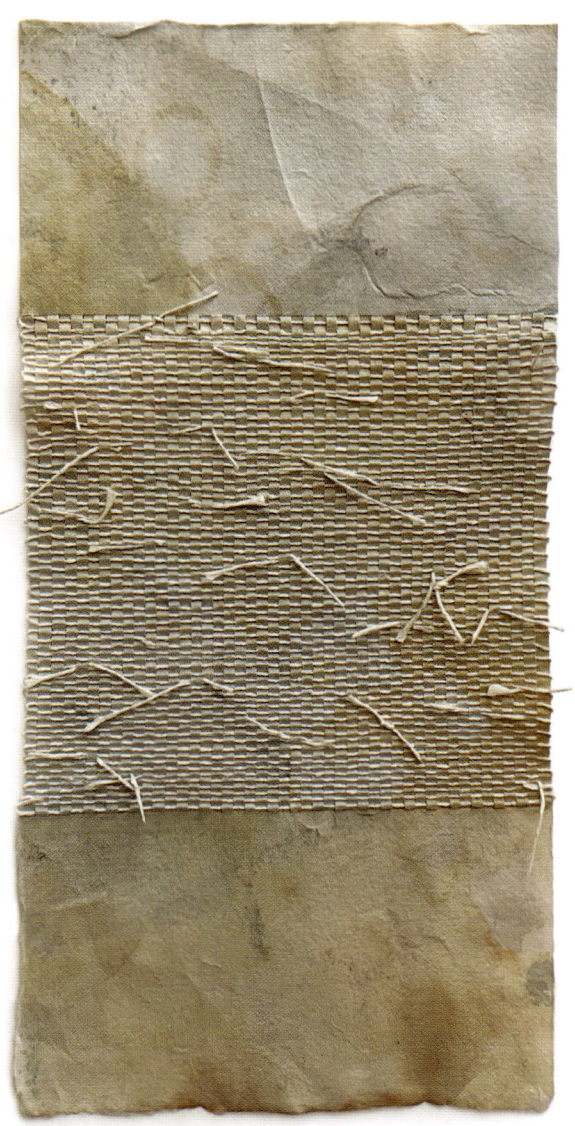

Julie VonDerVellen. *Beach Glass*, 2022. 12" × 6". Handmade paper, watercolor. Handwoven. *Photo courtesy of Julie VonDerVellen. www.JulieVonDer Vellen.com*

Carol Eaton. *Newspaper Yarn Weaving*, 2023. 13" × 6". Cotton yarn warp, newspaper, cotton yarn weft. Handwoven. *Photo courtesy of Nate Castner.*

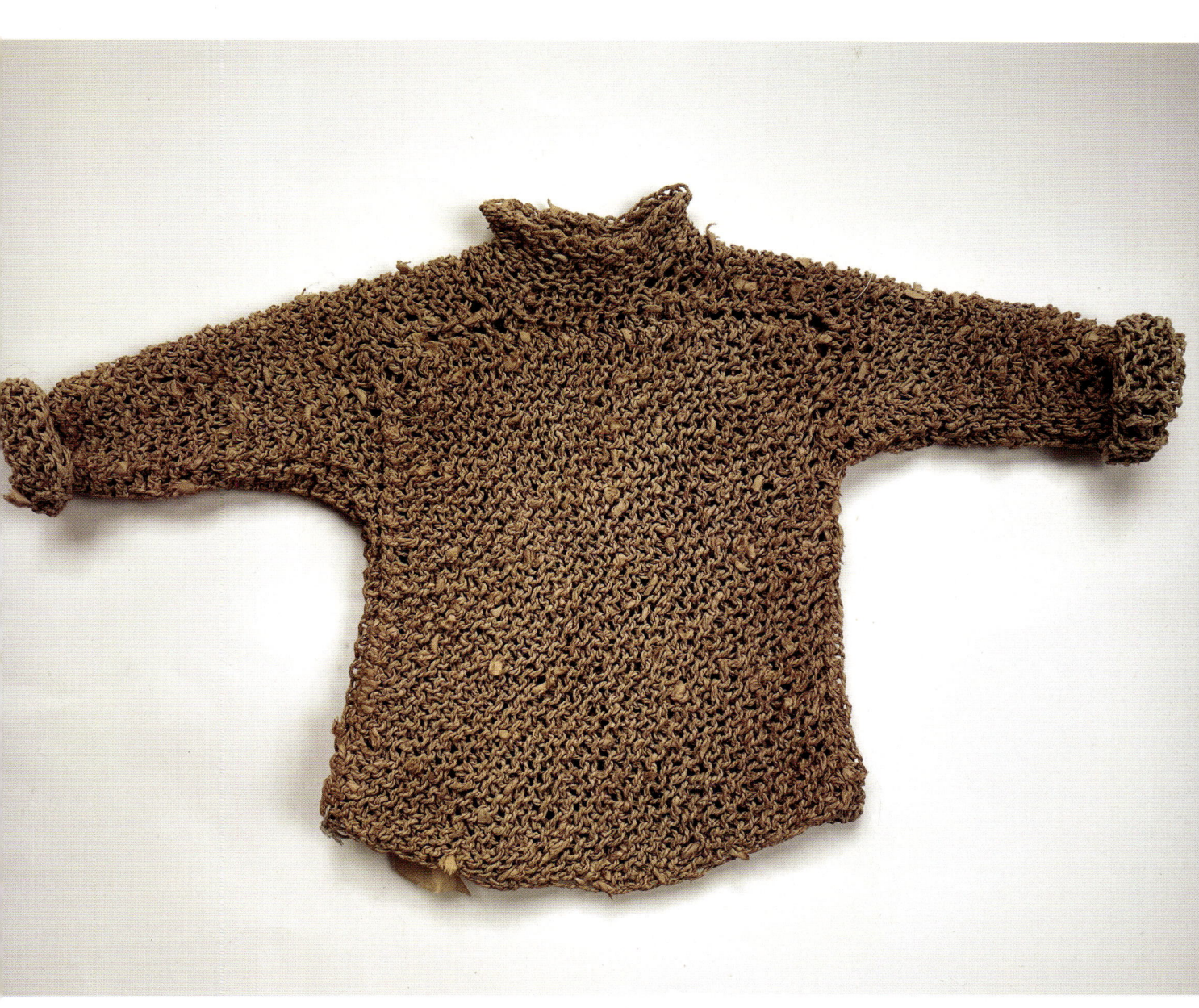

Sarah C. Swett. *Paper Pullover #3*, 2020. 10" × 17" × 1". Hand-spun used coffee filters. Hand knitting. *Photo courtesy of Sarah C. Swett*.

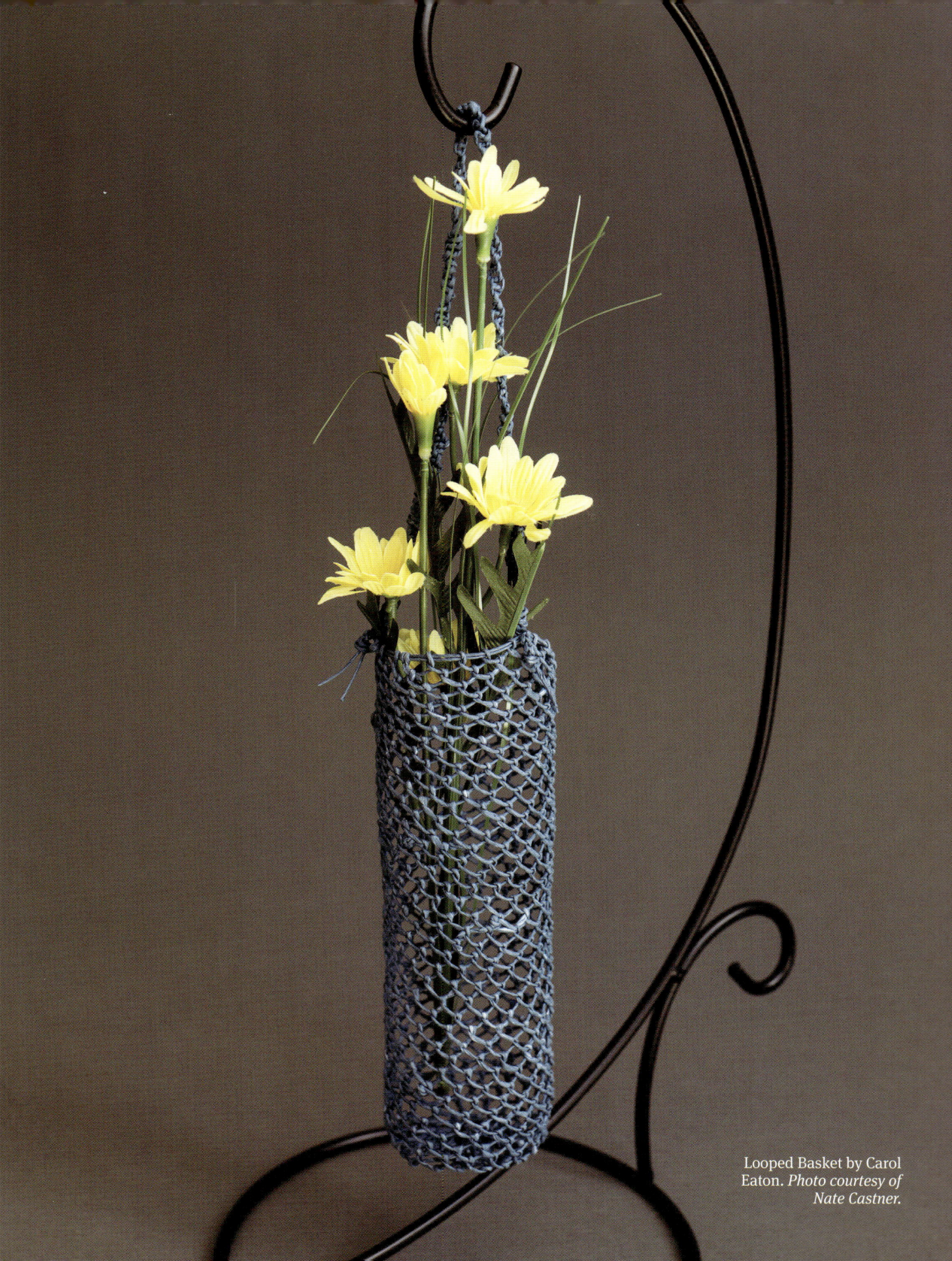

Looped Basket by Carol Eaton. *Photo courtesy of Nate Castner.*

Looped Basket

BY CAROL EATON

Skill Level: Intermediate

SUPPLIES

- medium-weight paper twine, approx. 60 yards, any color
- 1 foam pool noodle, 2¼ in. diameter
- 1 large-eye blunt darning needle
- 1 T pin

INSTRUCTIONS

1. Wrap a length of paper twine around the pool noodle twice and tie it off with a simple knot. Secure with a T pin. This is the top of your basket.

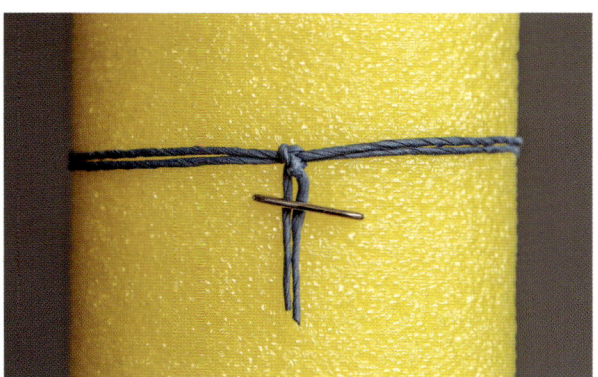

Step 1: Wrapping the twine and securing it with a T pin.
Step photos courtesy of Nate Castner.

2. To begin your first row of loops, cut a separate length of paper yarn approximately 24 inches long. Using a simple knot, tie one end of the new piece to the paper yarn already in place, then thread the needle with the other end of the yarn.

3. Slip the needle behind the two strands of paper twine, then place the needle on top of the yarn loop you just made. Pull the needle and twine to create a loop (which is technically a half-hitch knot). Continue to make the first row of loops. Try to keep the size of each loop about the same. If you run out of paper twine, cut another length and tie the two ends together.

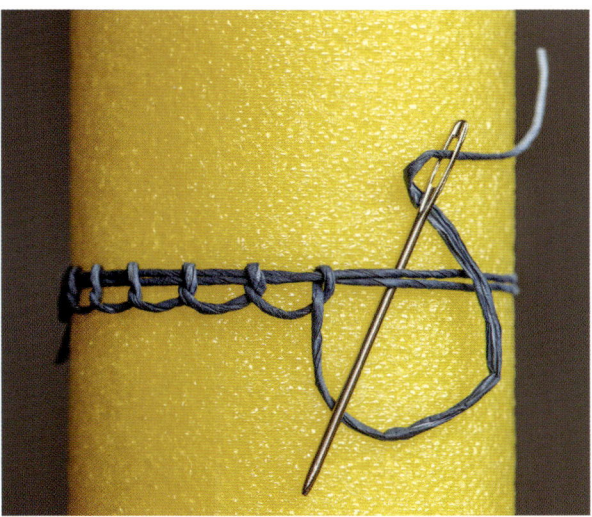

Step 1: Wrapping the twine and securing it with a T pin.

4 After you have finished your first row of loops, you will begin to make your second and all subsequent rows. To do this, place your needle under the loop above, working from the top down. As in Step 3, place the needle on top of the twine loop you just made and pull the needle and twine to create a loop.

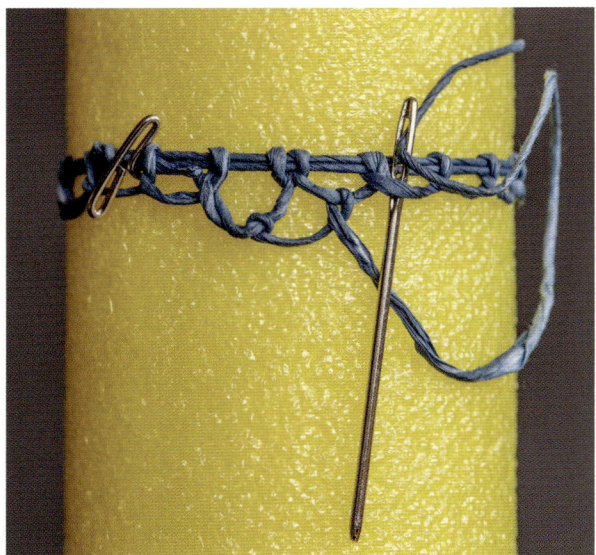

Step 4: Beginning to make the second row of loops.

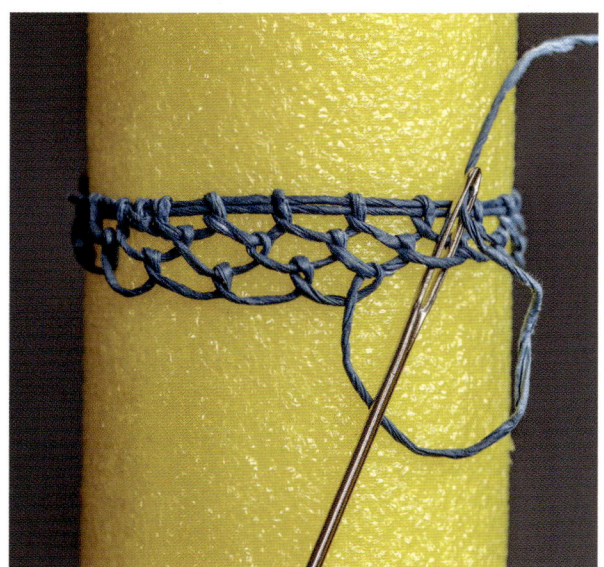

Step 4: Making more rows of loops.

5 Continue to make rows in this fashion until you reach the bottom of the pool noodle.

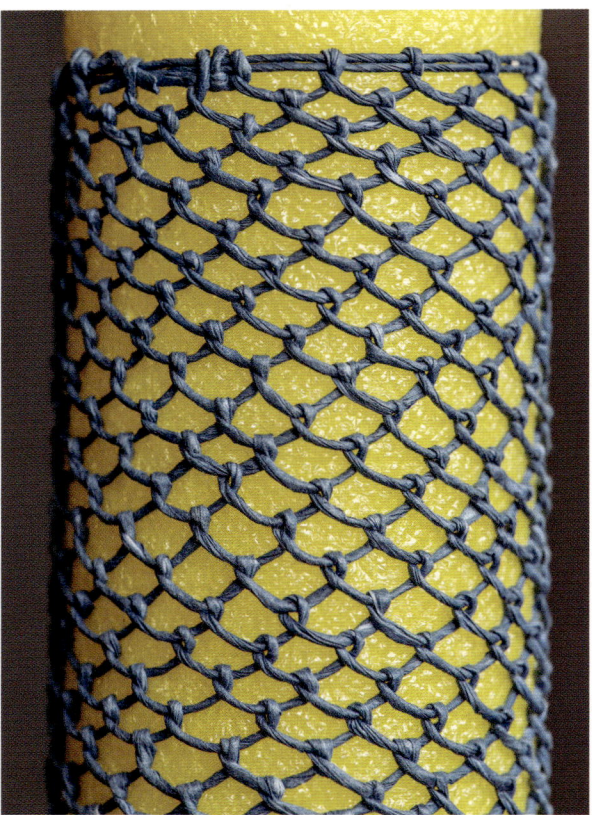

Step 5: Continuing to make more rows of loops.

6 Make smaller and smaller loops for the next few rows as you cover the bottom of the pool noodle. When you have covered the bottom, cut the working end of the twine and tie it to the nearest loop with a simple knot. Use the darning needle to weave all loose ends into the basket so that you cannot see them.

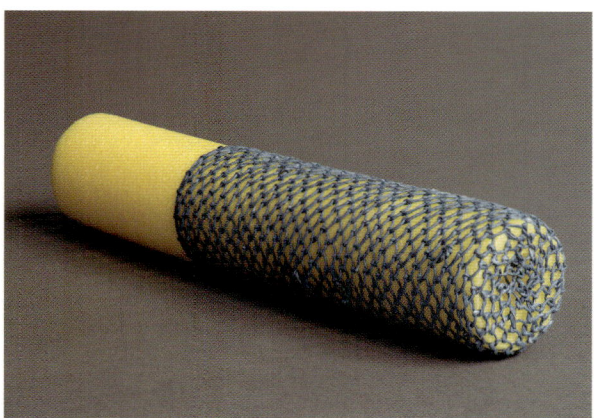

Step 6: Making smaller and smaller loops to cover the bottom of the pool noodle.

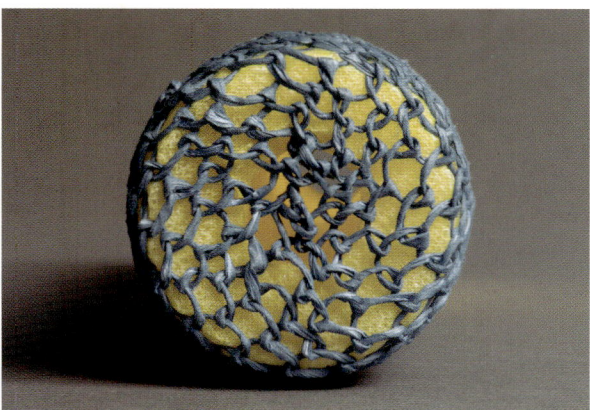

Step 6: Securing the end of the twine to the bottom of the pool noodle.

7 Slide the basket gently off the pool noodle.

8 This step is optional. If you wish, create a strap for hanging the basket in whatever way you choose. For example, you could tie a single strand of the paper twine to each side of the basket, making sure the ends of the strap are opposite one another. Or, you could knot a few strands of the paper twine together for a thicker strap and tie the ends to the basket. You may even wish to make a strap from a piece of fabric or leather. The choice is yours!

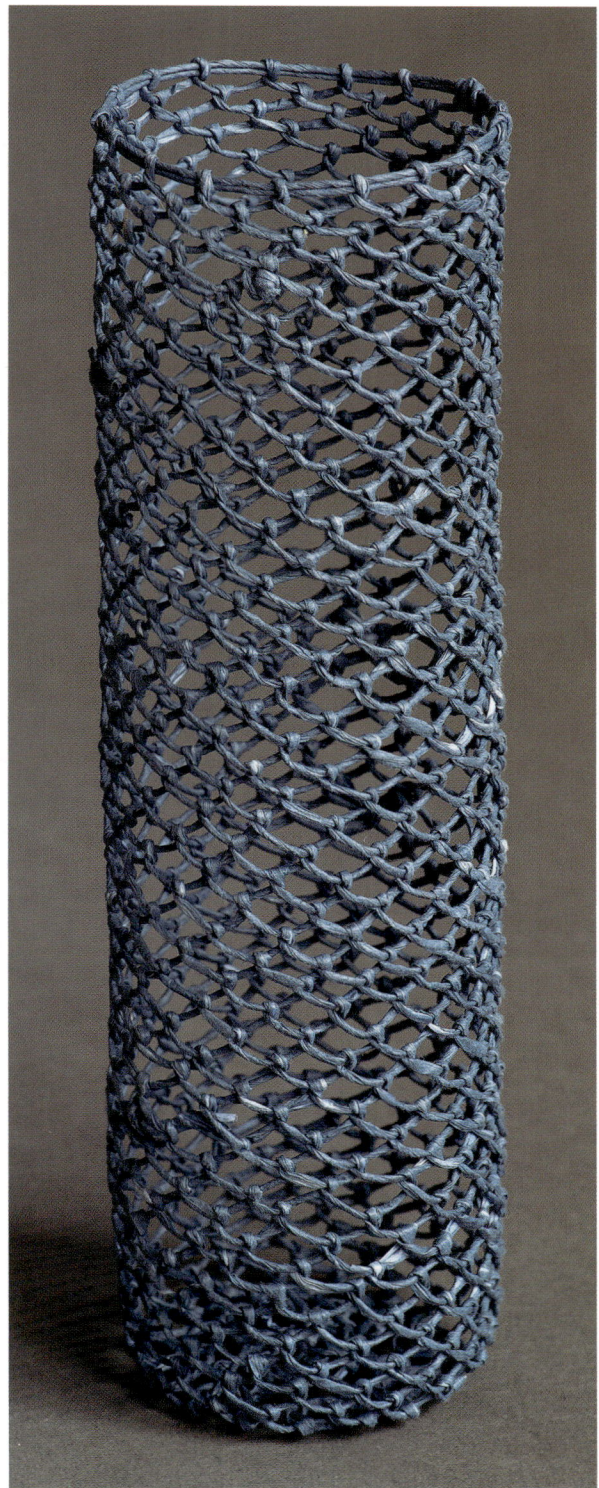

Step 7: Basket after sliding it off the pool noodle.

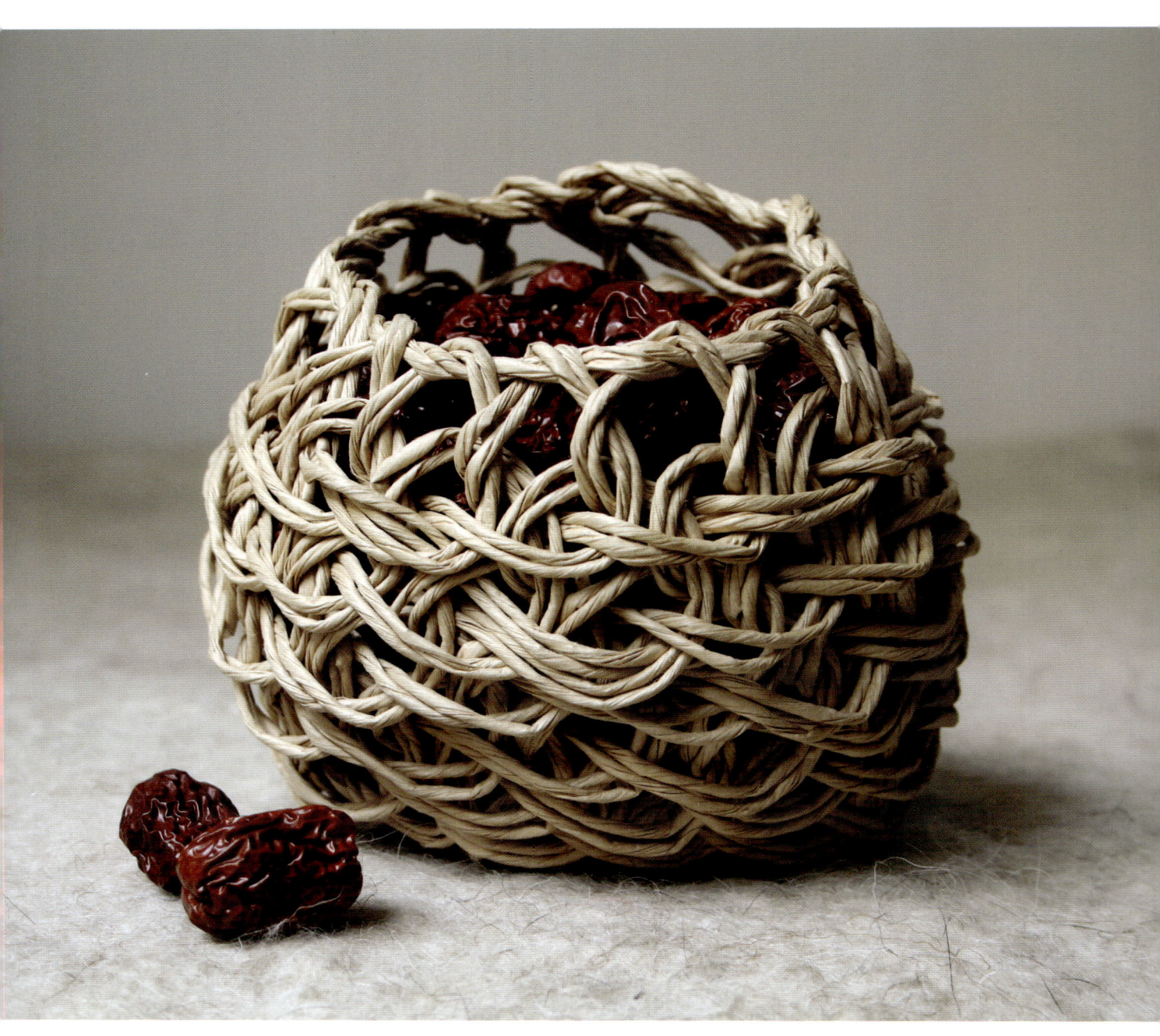

Kim Soon Ja. *Nutcase S Basket*, 2009. 4.7" (diameter). One hundred percent recycled paper. Macrame. *Photo courtesy of Corinne Muller & Piotr Oleszkowicz (Best Before). www.bestbefore.fr*

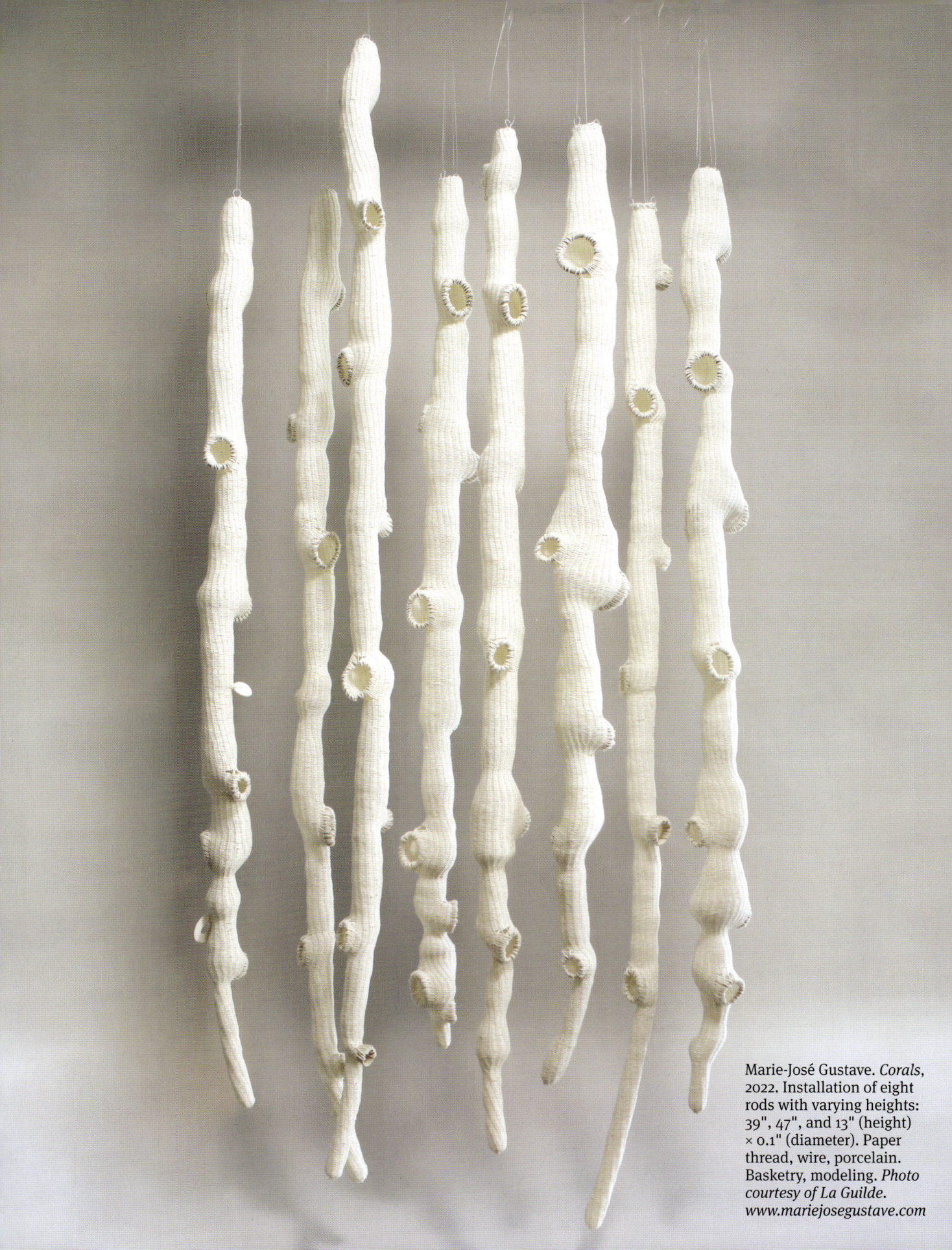

Marie-José Gustave. *Corals,* 2022. Installation of eight rods with varying heights: 39", 47", and 13" (height) × 0.1" (diameter). Paper thread, wire, porcelain. Basketry, modeling. *Photo courtesy of La Guilde. www.mariejosegustave.com*

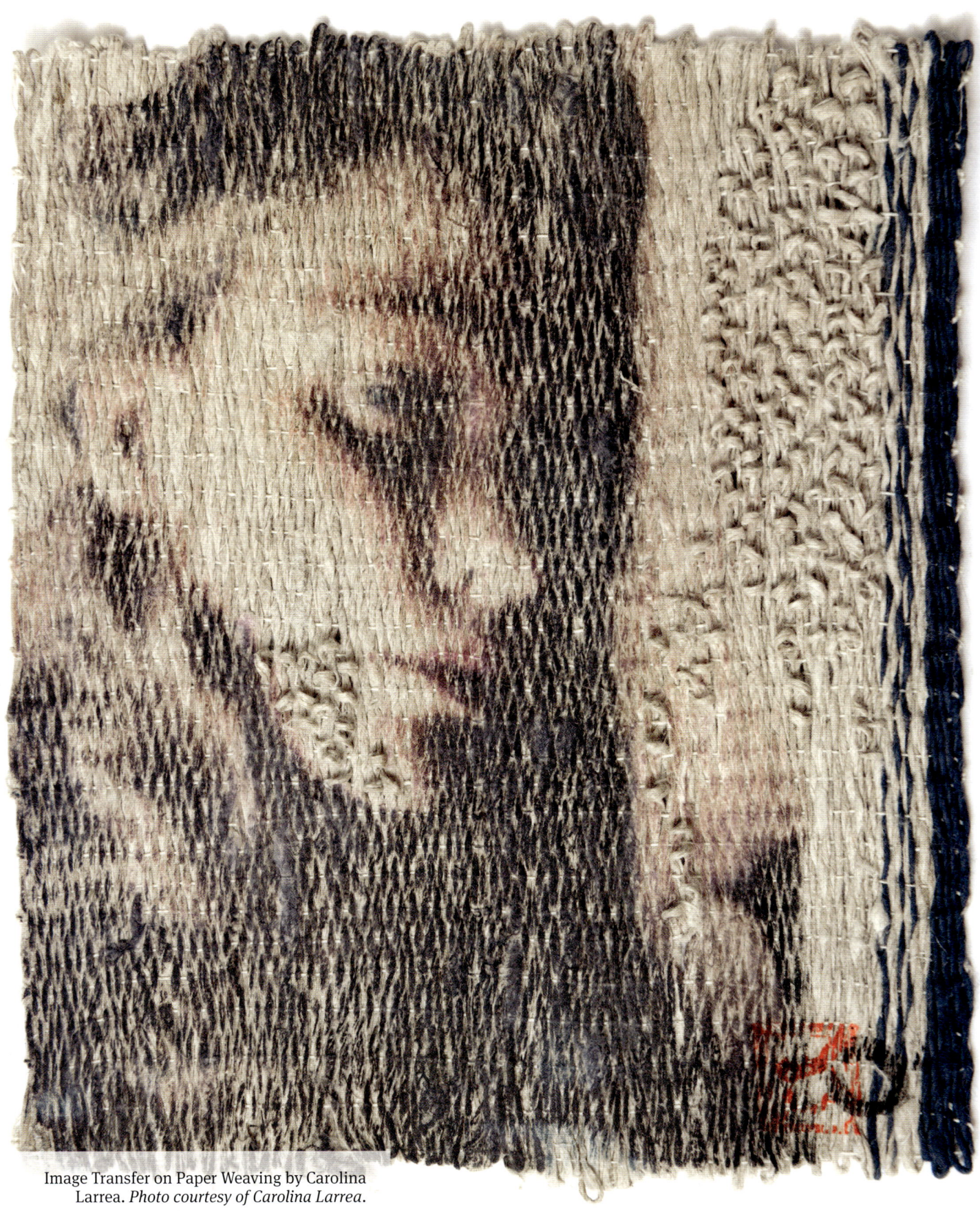

Image Transfer on Paper Weaving by Carolina
Larrea. *Photo courtesy of Carolina Larrea.*

Image Transfer on Paper Weaving

BY CAROLINA LARREA | CAROLINALARREA.COM

Skill Level: Experienced

SUPPLIES

- *kami-ito*, approx. 500 yards

- 1 hand loom, to accommodate a 4" × 6" woven piece

- cotton or linen thread

- paper or plastic protective cover for work surface

- 1 photocopied image

- 1 sheet of laser transparency film

- rubber gloves

- 1 container acetone solvent

- several cotton makeup remover pads

- 1 wooden spoon

- a weight, such as a wooden cutting board

- 1 acid free glue stick

- several thin bamboo sticks or toothpicks

- 1 sewing needle

- 1 personalized Japanese hanko chop (name stamp) and ink, *or* a permanent marker

- 1 piece of matboard, 4" × 6", or cut to the size of the woven paper

INSTRUCTIONS

1. Copy image onto the sheet of laser transparency film. Set it aside.

2. Prepare the warp with cotton thread. (Linen thread can also be used for this purpose, although linen thread is more rigid.)

3. Weave the *kami-ito* through the warp.

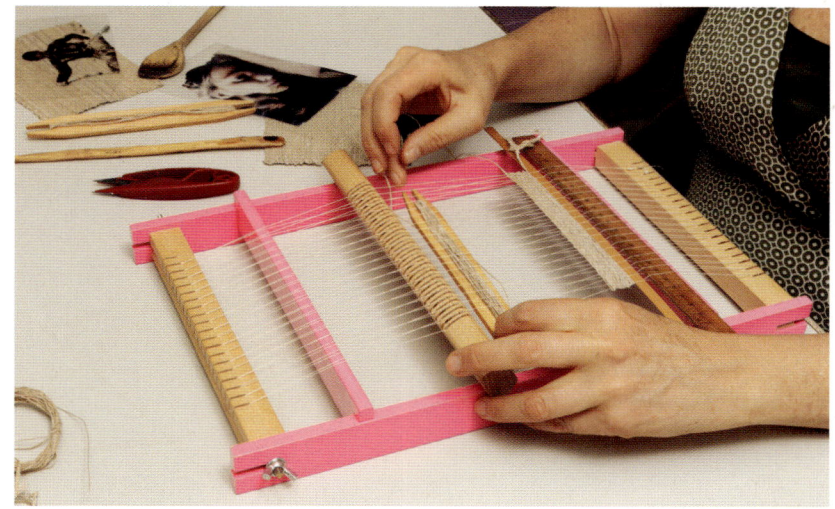

Step 3: Weaving the *kami-ito* through the warp. *Step photos courtesy of Carolina Larrea.*

4. When you have finished weaving the paper, you can transfer your image onto it. Place paper or plastic sheeting on your work surface to protect it. Make sure there are no wrinkles in the plastic sheeting; this can result in an unexpected mark on your image.

5. Remove the woven paper from the loom and place it on the paper or plastic sheeting. Then, using a cotton pad, dampen it with acetone. *Note:* Conduct this step in a well-ventilated area because the acetone not only has a very strong odor, but it is also volatile (in other words, potentially explosive). Work with care.

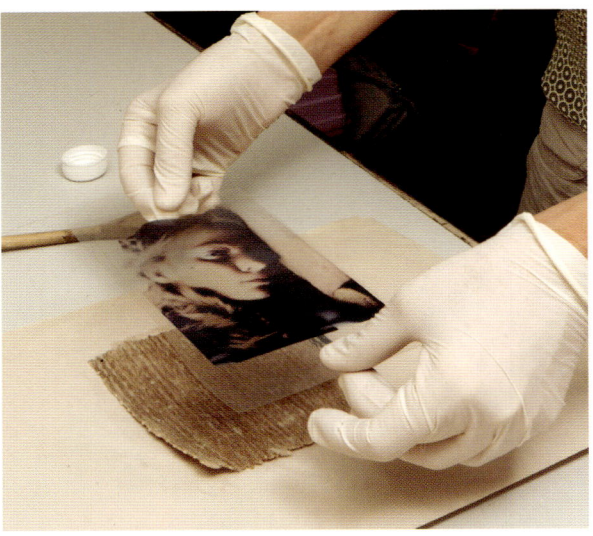

Step 6: Preparing to place the image ink-side down onto the woven paper.

7. Press a cotton pad carefully and evenly over the entire photocopy. This process begins to transfer the ink of the image to the woven paper.

8. Switch the cotton pad for a wooden spoon, and continue to press and rub the image into the woven paper.

9. After 30 seconds, lift a corner of the transparency film a tiny bit to check whether the image has been transferred. If not, continue rubbing.

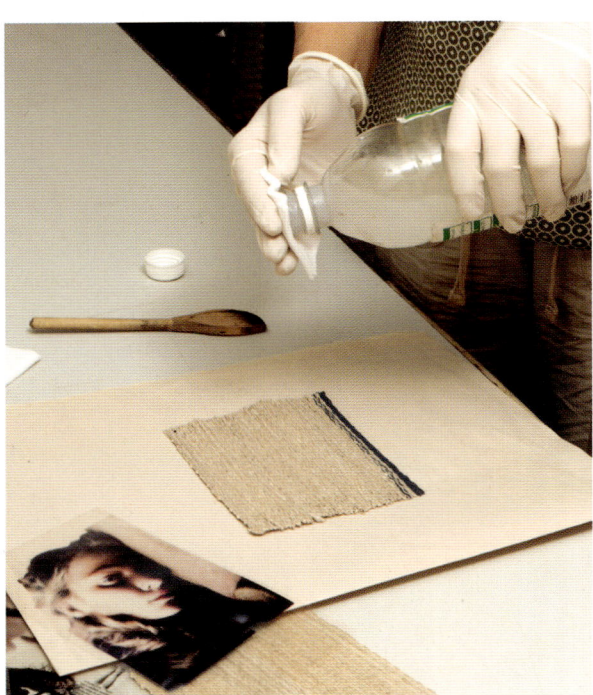

Step 5: Preparing the woven paper for image transfer.

6. Place the photocopy ink-side down on the woven paper moistened with the solvent. Hold the image as still as possible.

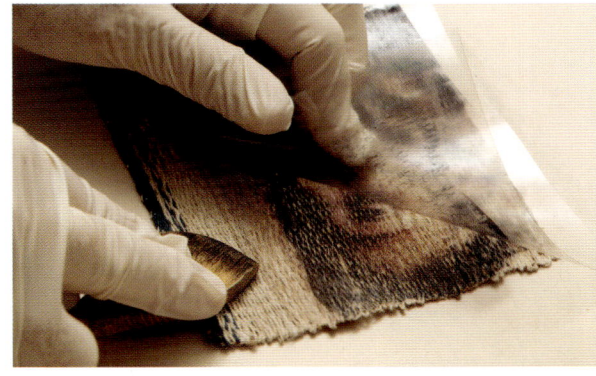

Step 9: Checking to determine whether the image has transferred to the woven paper.

10 Pull the transparency paper from the woven paper when the image has transferred completely to the woven paper.

11 Place the cutting board on top of the woven paper to help it maintain its shape as it dries.

12 To add texture to your piece, you can create raised loops of thread. Choose the area where you want to create the loops and grab your needle and thread, and skewers or toothpicks. To make the loops, you can use *kami-ito* or any other thread or yarn. Place skewers on top of the image and sew loops around them as desired. Fasten the thread or yarn by making a knot at the back of the piece. Weave in all ends.

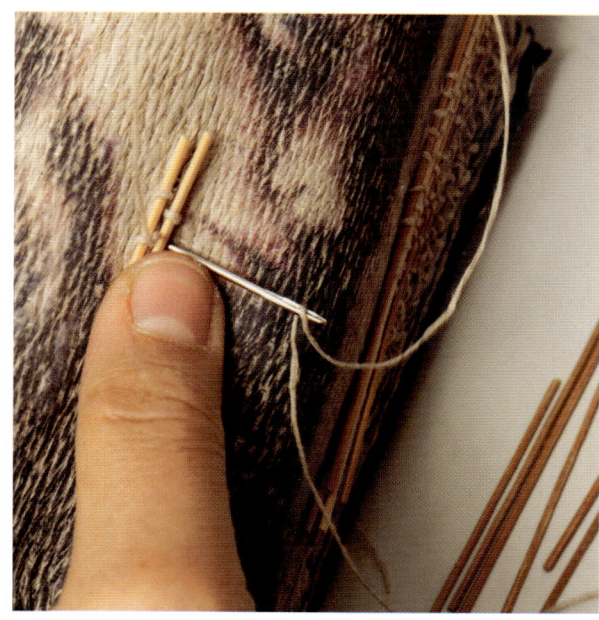

Step 12: Creating multiple loops on the image.

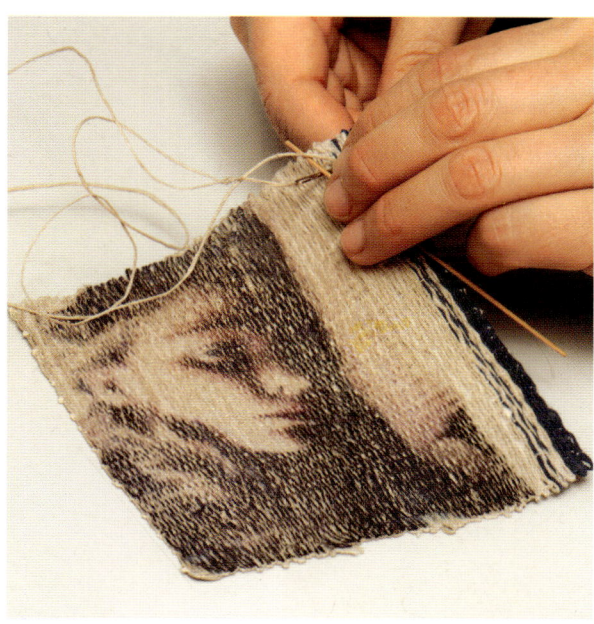

Step 12: Creating raised loops on the image.

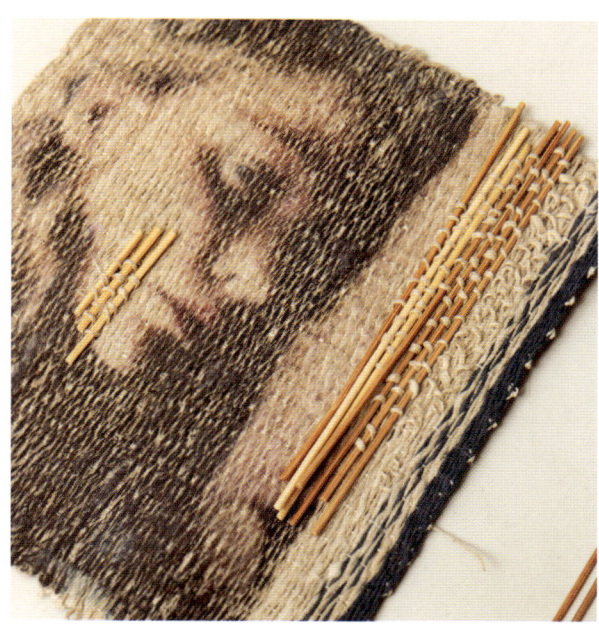

Step 12: Completed multiple raised loops scattered on top of the image, with skewers in place.

Project 8: Image Transfer on Paper Weaving | 77

13 Take the skewers out slowly, one by one.

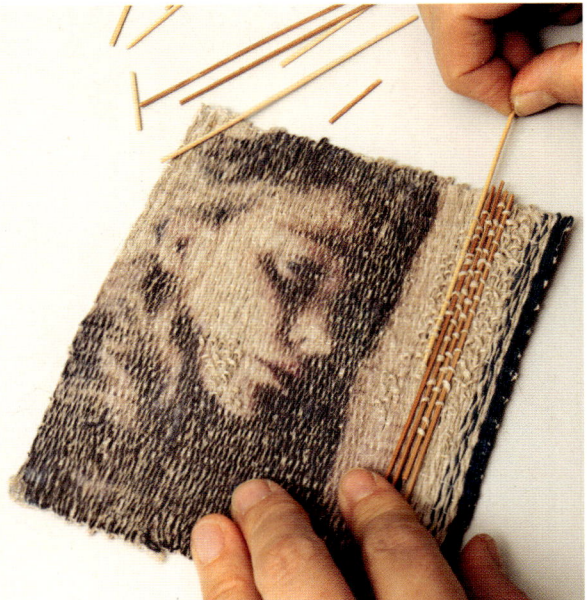

Step 13: Removing the skewers one by one.

14 Reinforce the back of the woven paper with the piece of matboard cut to size. To do so, apply glue to the back of the woven paper using the acid-free glue stick. Then, adhere the paper to the matboard.

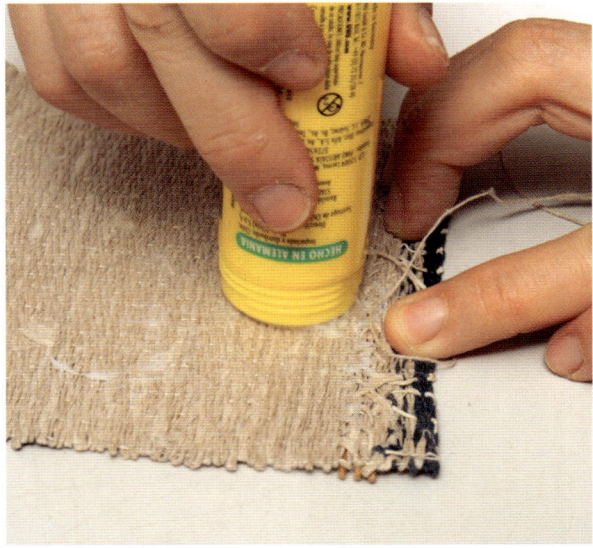

Step 14: Applying glue to the back of the woven paper in preparation to adhering the matboard.

15 Sign your work with your hanko chop or marker.

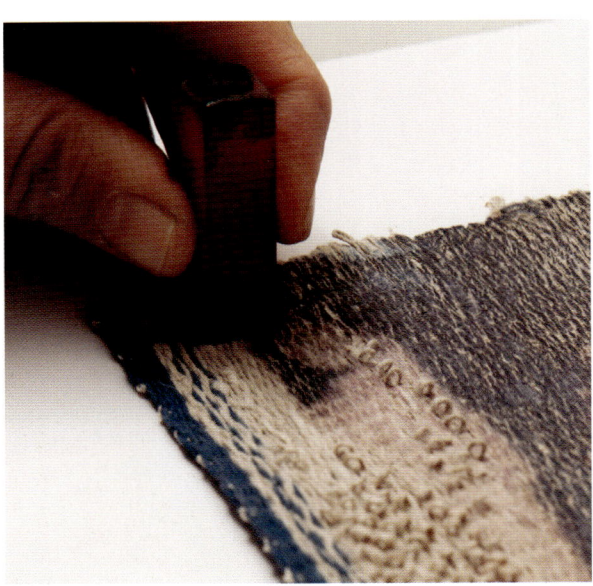

Step 15: Signing your work.

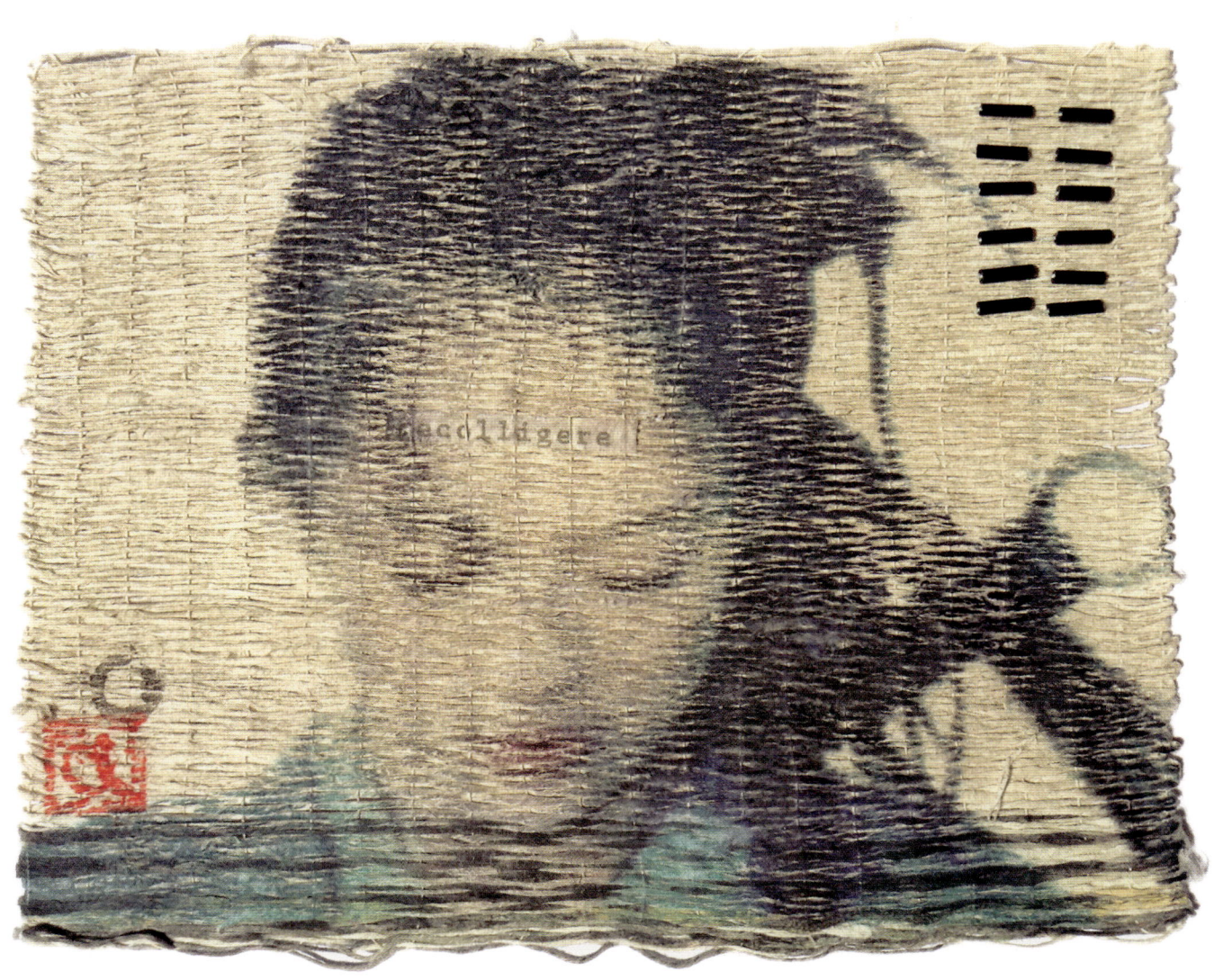

Carolina Larrea. *Recolligere*, 2015. 5.9" × 4.5". Japanese paper thread, image. Image transferred onto handwoven thread.
Photo courtesy of Carolina Larrea. www.carolinalarrea.com

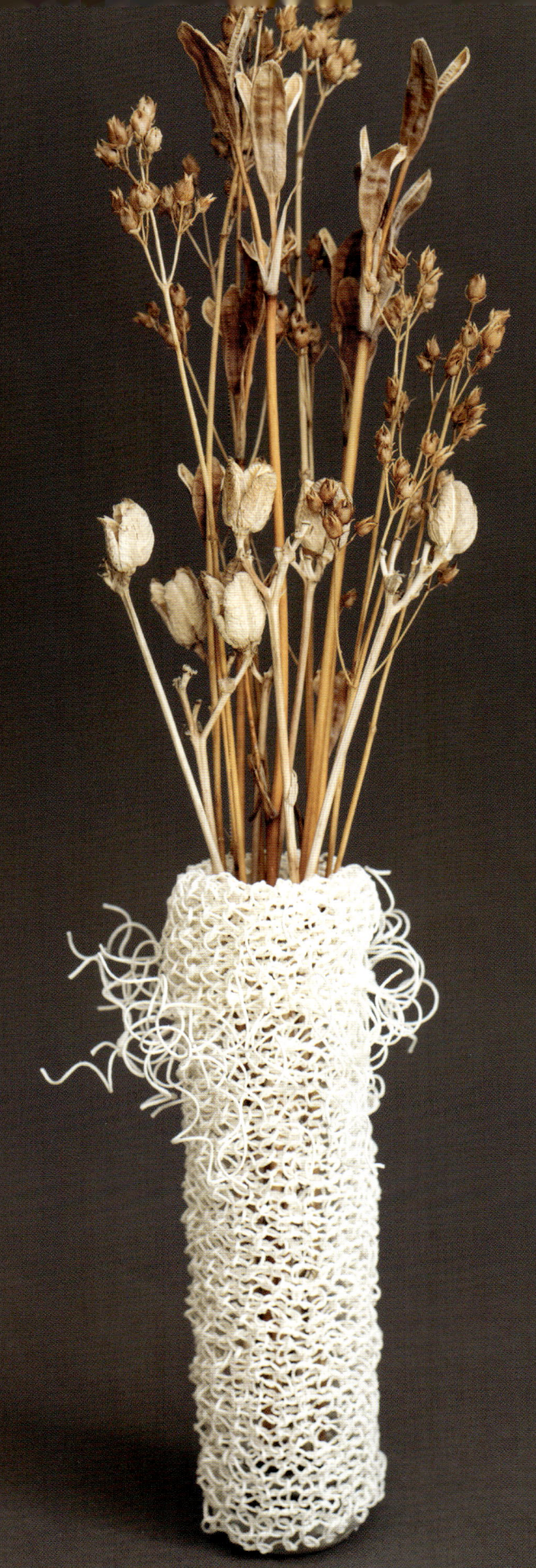

Knitted Vase Cover by
Barbara Olson. *Photo
courtesy of Nate Castner.*

Knitted Vase Cover

BY BARBARA OLSON | BARBARAOLSON.NET

Skill Level: Experienced

SUPPLIES

- medium paper yarn, approx. 1,200 yards (mine is from paperphine.com)

- 1 pair US size 6 knitting needles

- 1 large-eye blunt darning needle

- 1 glass cylinder vase, 8" high × 5" diameter

INSTRUCTIONS FOR VASE

1. Cast on 44 stitches.

2. Work in garter stitch (knit every row) until piece measures 6 inches or is long enough to wrap around the vase. Cast off.

3. With right sides together, matching the cast-off edge to the cast-on edge, slipstitch the edges together with the paper yarn.

4. The yarn tube will be longer than the vase. Fold down the top edge to match the height of the vase.

INSTRUCTIONS FOR FRINGE

1. Cut 28 pieces of 8-inch long yarn.

2. Use the darning needle to thread each piece of yarn into the bottom edge of the fold, spacing the fringe pieces evenly. Pull each piece of yarn halfway through the bottom edge of the fold so that each dangling piece is 4 inches. Tie a knot to secure each piece.

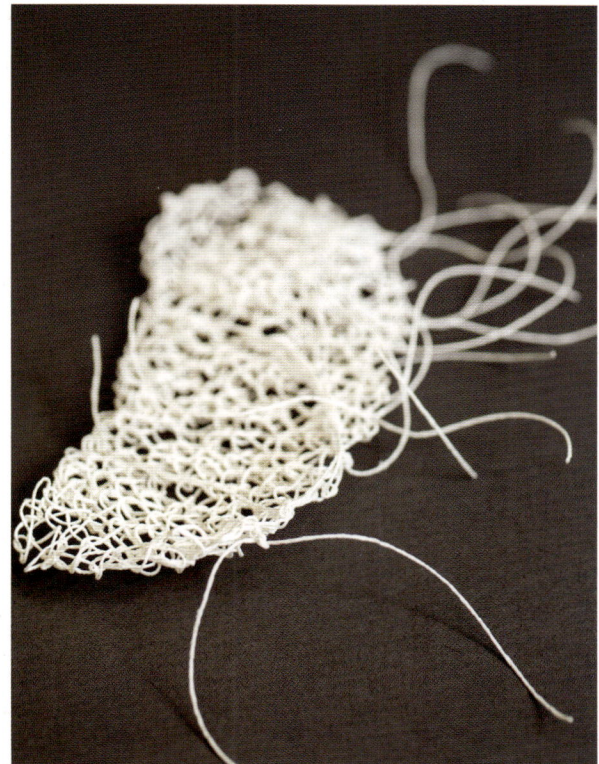

Step 2: Creating the fringe. *Step photos courtesy of Nate Castner.*

③ Wrap each double length of yarn around a knitting needle to curl it. The paper yarn will hold the curl.

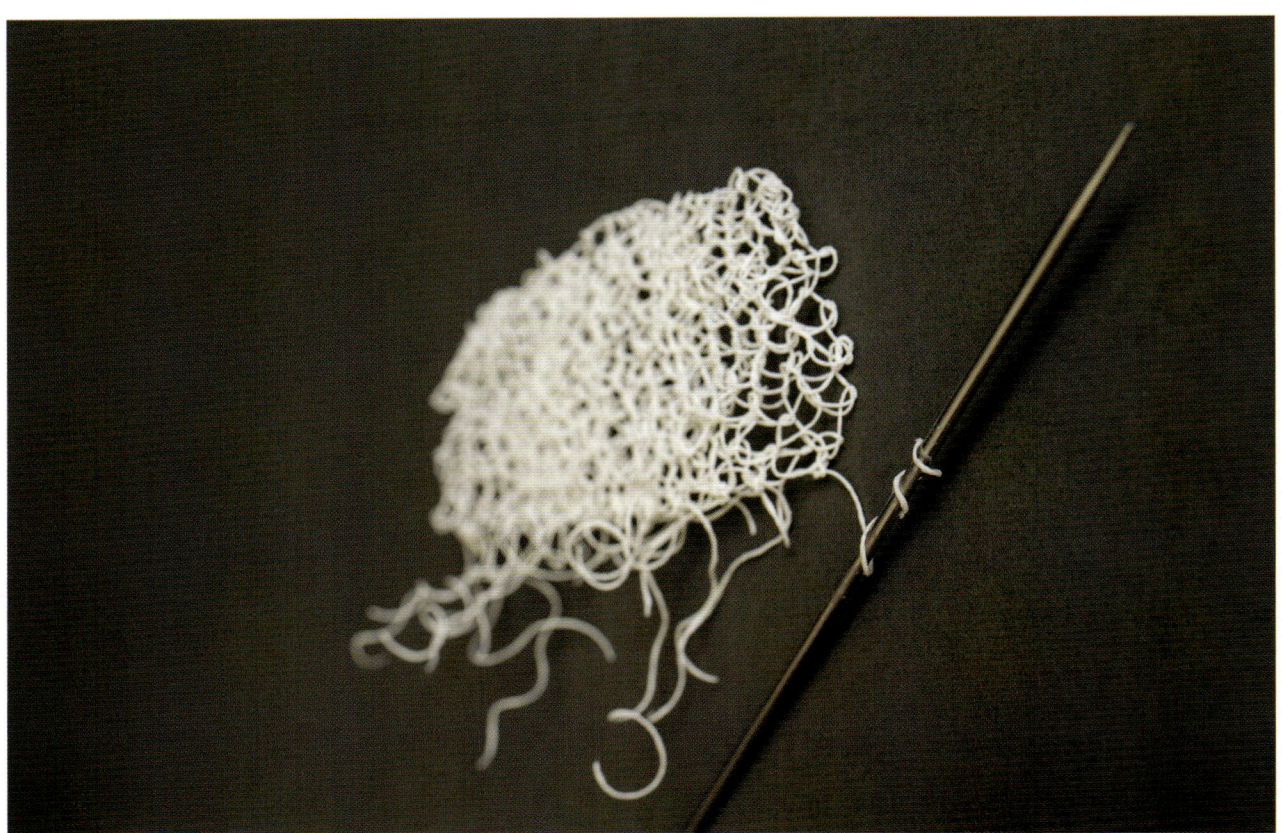

Step 3: Curling the fringe around a knitting needle.

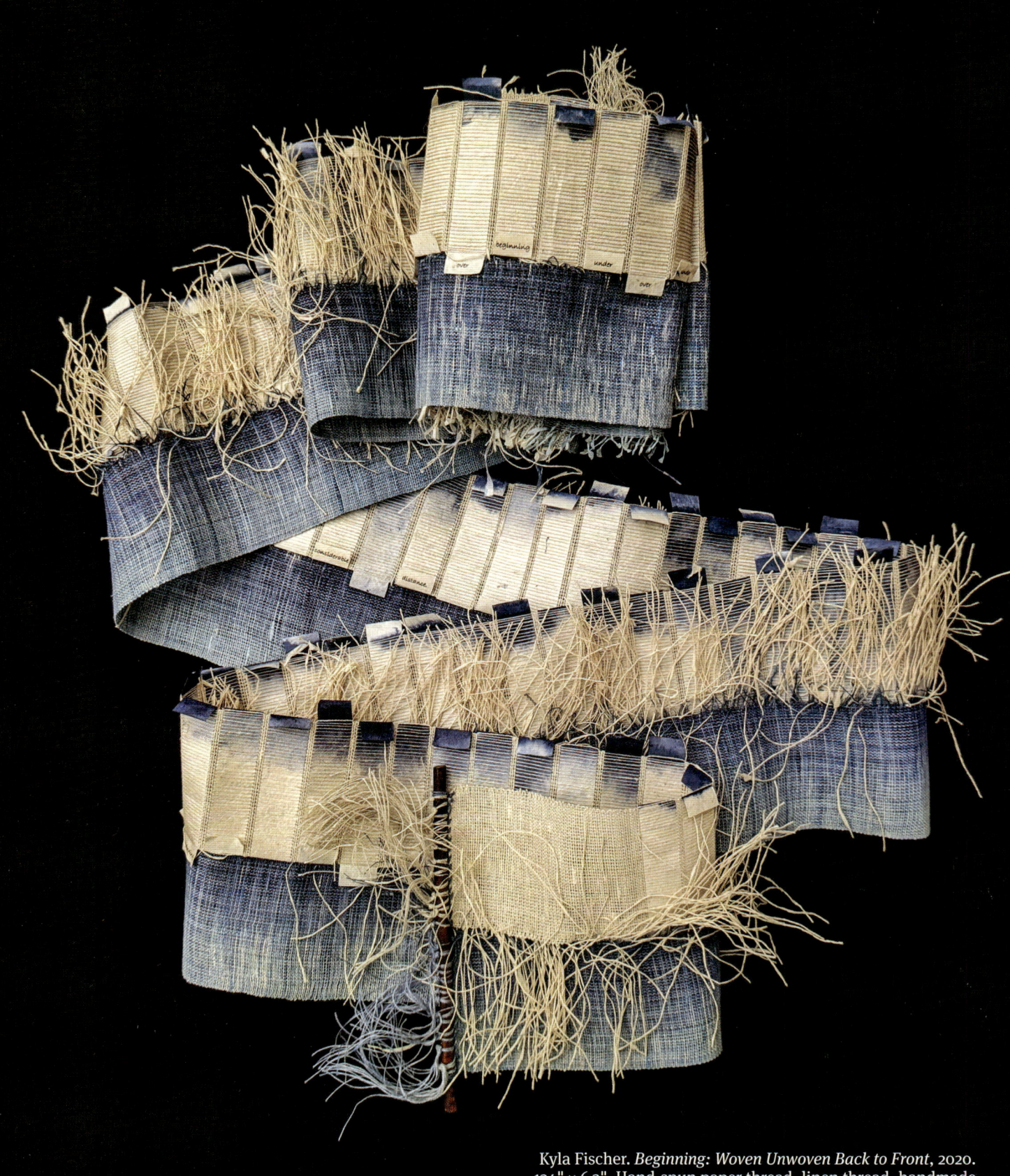

Kyla Fischer. *Beginning: Woven Unwoven Back to Front*, 2020. 134" × 6.3". Hand-spun paper thread, linen thread, handmade kozo paper, ink, dye. Handwoven. *Photo courtesy of Kyla Fischer. www.fischerk@telus.net*

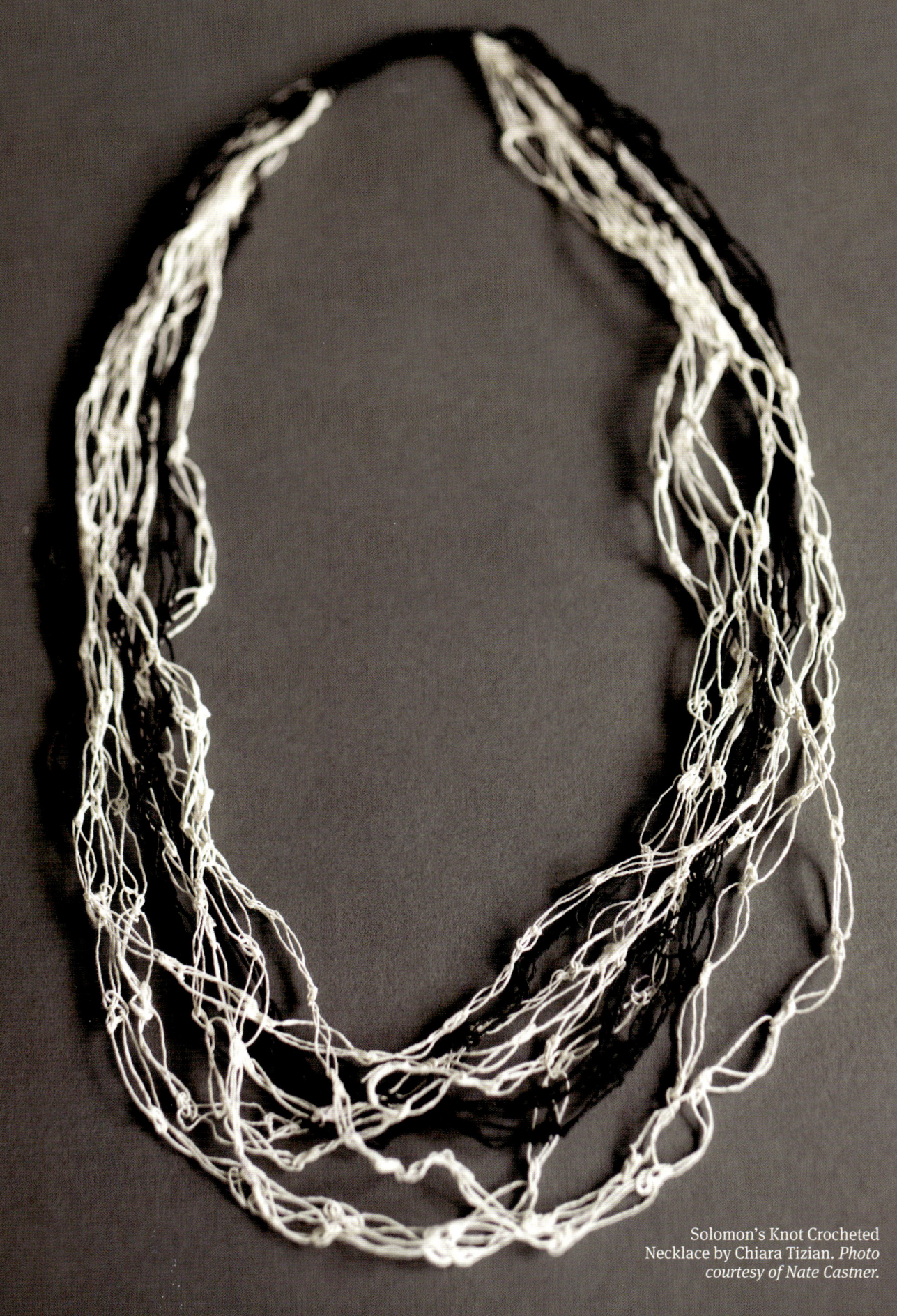

Solomon's Knot Crocheted Necklace by Chiara Tizian. *Photo courtesy of Nate Castner.*

Solomon's Knot Crocheted Necklace

BY CHIARA TIZIAN | CHIARATIZIAN.COM

Skill Level: Experienced

SUPPLIES

- handmade or purchased *kami-ito*, approx. 10 yards, of the thickness and colors of your choice

- 1 3-mm crochet hook

- 1 large-eye blunt darning needle

- *konjac* paste made from powder or diluted wallpaper glue (*optional*) (see page 30)

INSTRUCTIONS

This necklace is made of multiple strands of *kami-ito* and Solomon's knot crochet stitches. It uses two black strands and six white strands.

1. Chain 2.

2. Single crochet in the first chain, so that you have one loop on your hook.

3. Yarn over and pull through as in a regular chain stitch.

4. Take a close look at your work. You should see a loop that has two strands in the front, closest to you, and another solo strand in the back. Insert your hook underneath the solo strand in the back of the work. Yarn over and draw through the first loop on your hook. There will be two more loops on the hook. Yarn over and pull through both of these remaining loops. You have completed a single Solomon's knot stitch.

5. To create a row of Solomon's knots, repeat Steps 3 and 4. For Step 3, take the last stitch created at the end of Step 4 and draw it up to the correct height.

6. Repeat Steps 3 and 4 until you reach the chosen length of your strand. *Note:* The strand should be long enough, when connected, to fit over your head.

7. Fasten the ends of the strand with a slip stitch.

8. Make as many strands as you want for your necklace.

9. To join the strands and secure them, cut a long piece of *kami-ito*, align the 2 chains of each strand, and wrap the yarn around the chain stitches to cover and fasten them.

10 Use a darning needle to weave the tails under the wrapped yarn.

Note: Depending on the type and thickness of *kami-ito* you are using, the strands could twist a bit. You can consider this a feature or you can choose to minimize it. To do the latter, lay the necklace on a blocking mat or other pinable surface, moisten it with *konjac* paste, and block the strands with rust-proof pins. The necklace will keep its shape when it dries.

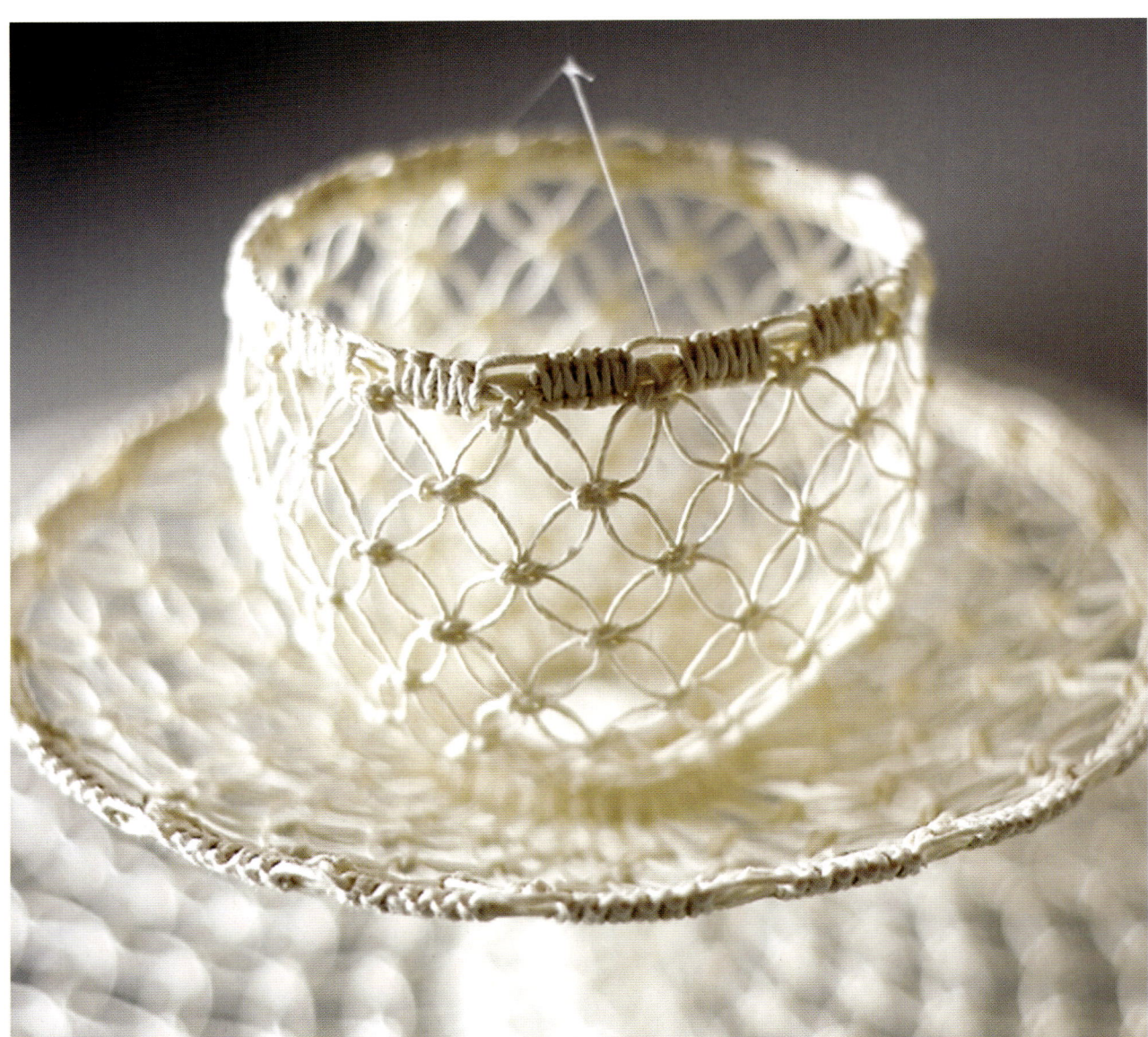

Nithikul Nimkulrat. *The Coffee Cup*, 2006. 2.8" × 5.9" × 5.9". Finnish paper yarn. Hand-knotted. *Photo courtesy of Phakphum Julnipitawong. www.nithikul.com*

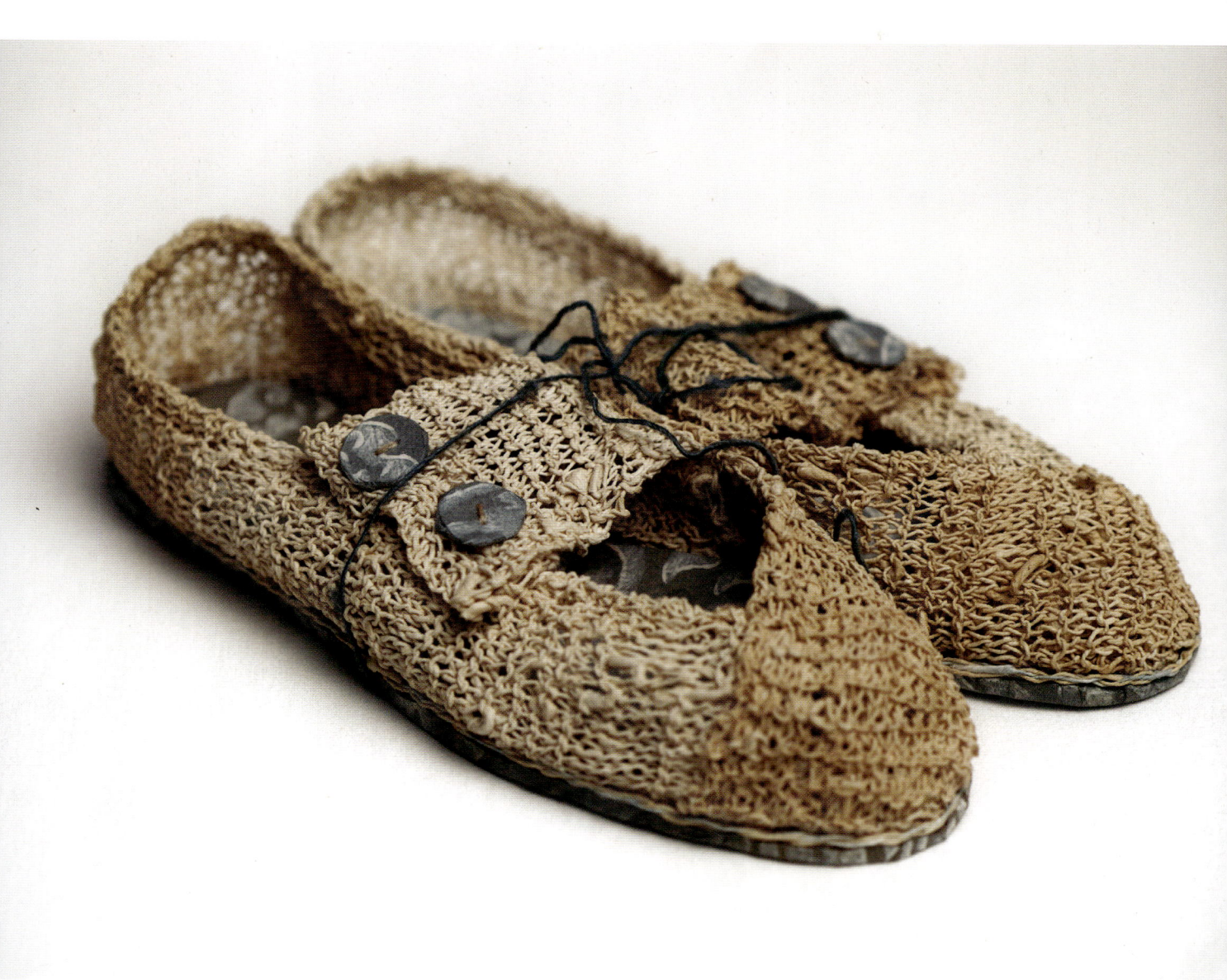

Chiara Tizian. *Sia Lieve il Tuo Passo* (*Paper Shoes*), 2018. 6.5" × 7.5" × 2.5". Handspun Korean mulberry *hanji* paper yarn, ancient wallpaper (sole). Plant-dyed and hand-knitted. *Photo courtesy of Azzurra Galla. www.chiaratizian.com*

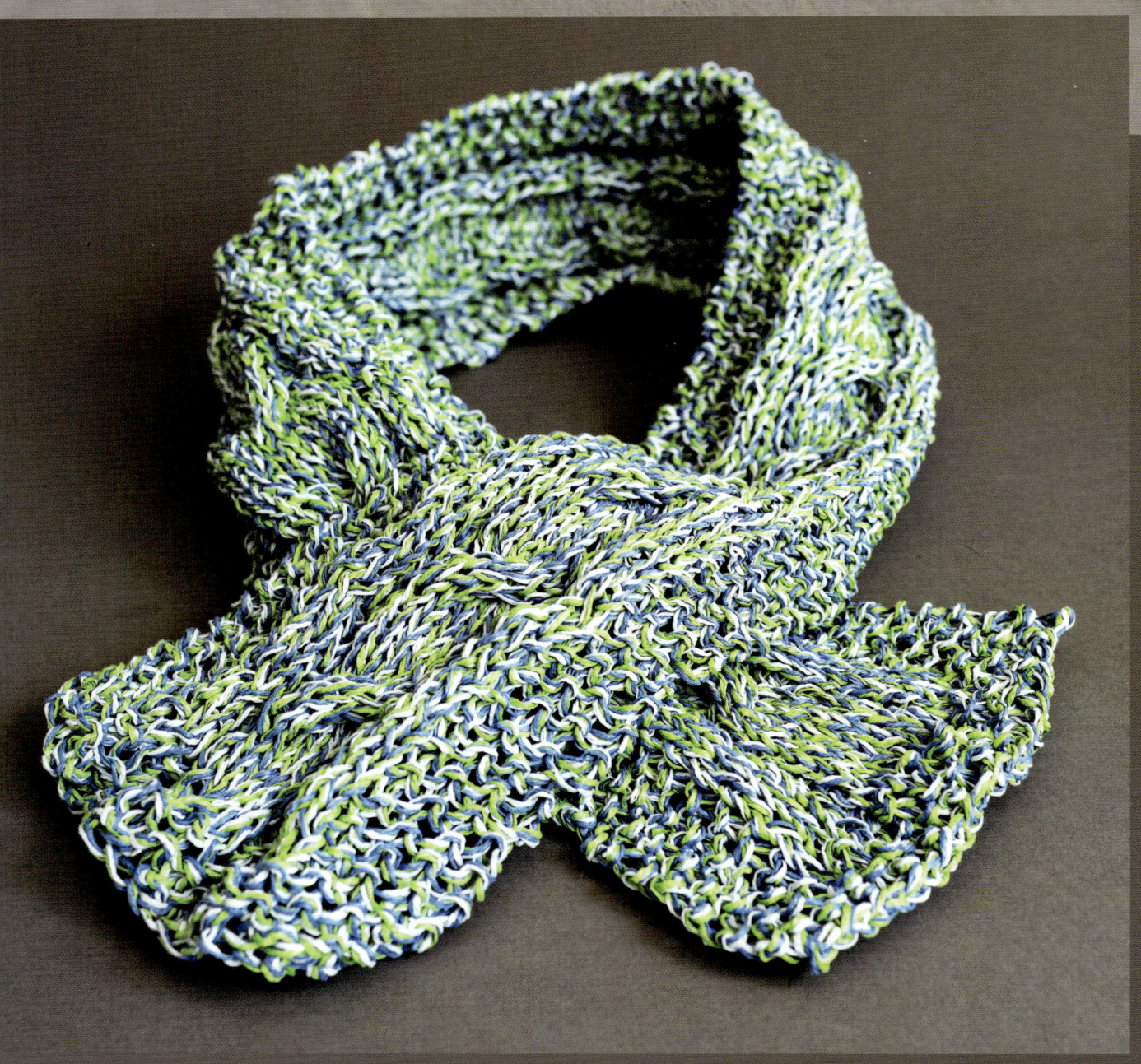

Knitted Cable Twine Scarf by Cat Ohala. *Photo courtesy of Nate Castner.*

Knitted Cable Twine Scarf

BY CAT OHALA

Skill Level: Experienced

SUPPLIES

- paper twine, approx. 800 yards (I used colors from paperphine.com)
- 1 pair US size 9 metal knitting needles (The

- needles must be metal; I snapped a pair of heavy-duty plastic needles.)
- 1 cable holder

- 1 large-eye blunt darning needle
- 1 pair of nonlatex fabric-lined rubber gloves

INSTRUCTIONS

You need very strong hands to work this project, and the rubber gloves are a lifesaver for your hands and fingers.

1. Cast on 24 stitches.

2. Row 1: Knit 1, purl 1 to end of row.

3. Row 2: Purl 1, knit 1 to end of row. These 2 rows create what is known as the seed stitch.

4. Rows 3 and 4: Repeat rows 1 and 2.

5. Row 5: (Knit 1, purl 1) 2 times, knit 3, purl 2, knit 6, purl 2, knit 3, (purl 1, knit 1) 2 times.

6. Row 6: (Purl 1, knit 1) 2 times, purl 3, knit 2, purl 6, knit 2, purl 3, (knit 1, purl 1) 2 times.

7. Rows 7, 9, 11, 13: As Row 5

8. Rows 8, 10, 12, 14: As Row 6

9. Row 15: (Knit 1, purl 1) 2 times, knit 3, purl 2. Place the next 3 stitches onto the cable holder and move it to the back of the work. Knit the next 3 stitches. Knit the 3 stitches from the cable holder. Purl 2, knit 3, (purl 1, knit 1) 2 times. *Note:* Knit the cable stitches loosely; there is no "give" (elasticity) to the paper yarn.

10. Row 16: (Purl 1, knit 1) 2 times, purl 3, knit 2, purl 6, knit 2, purl 3, (knit 1, purl 1) 2 times.

11. Repeat Rows 3–16 18 times.

12. Repeat Rows 5–14.

13. Repeat Rows 1–4 and tie off end.

14. Weave in all yarn ends using the darning needle.

Marie-José Gustave. *Roots*, 2020. 14" × 11". Paper, wire, red clay. Basketry. *Photo courtesy of Marie-José Gustave. www.mariejosegustave.com*

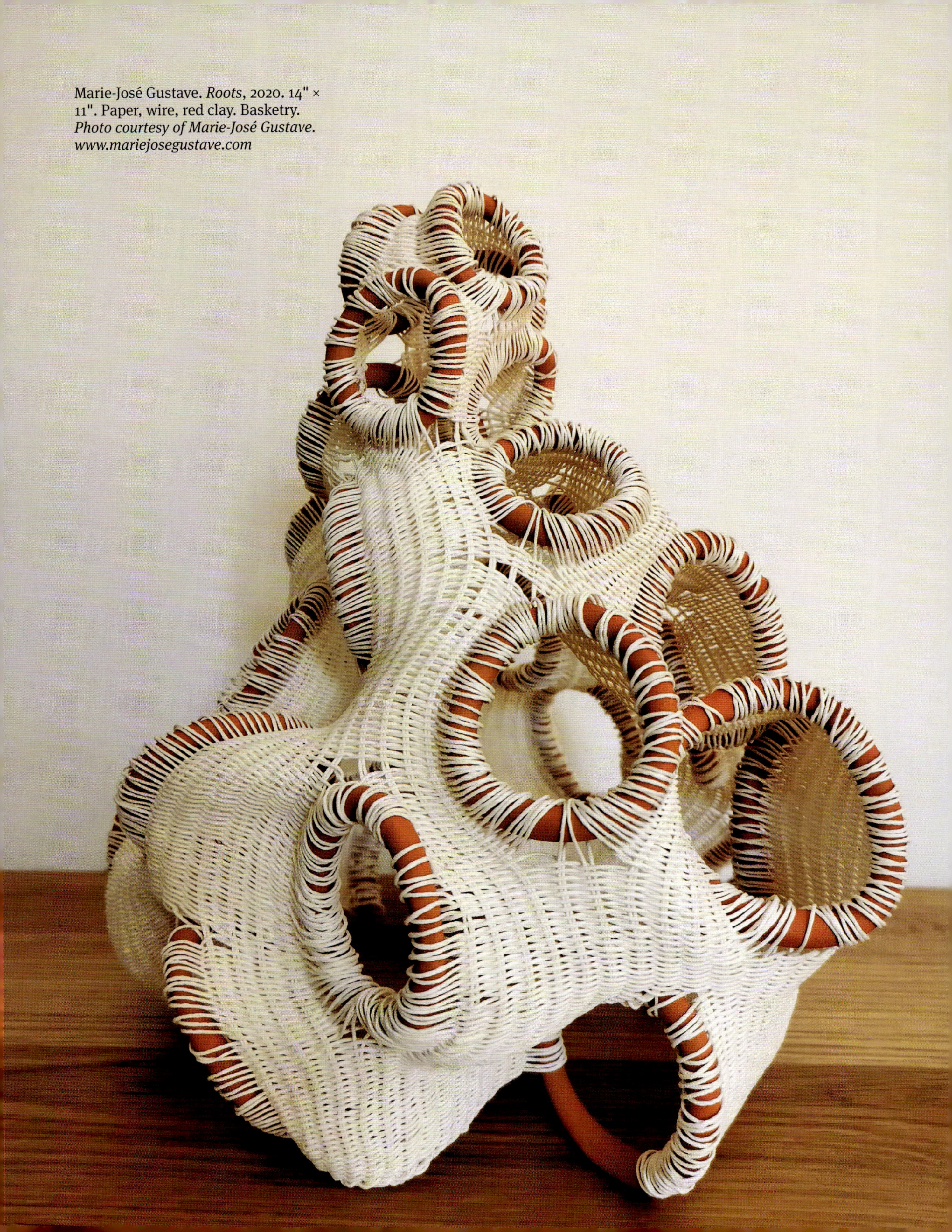

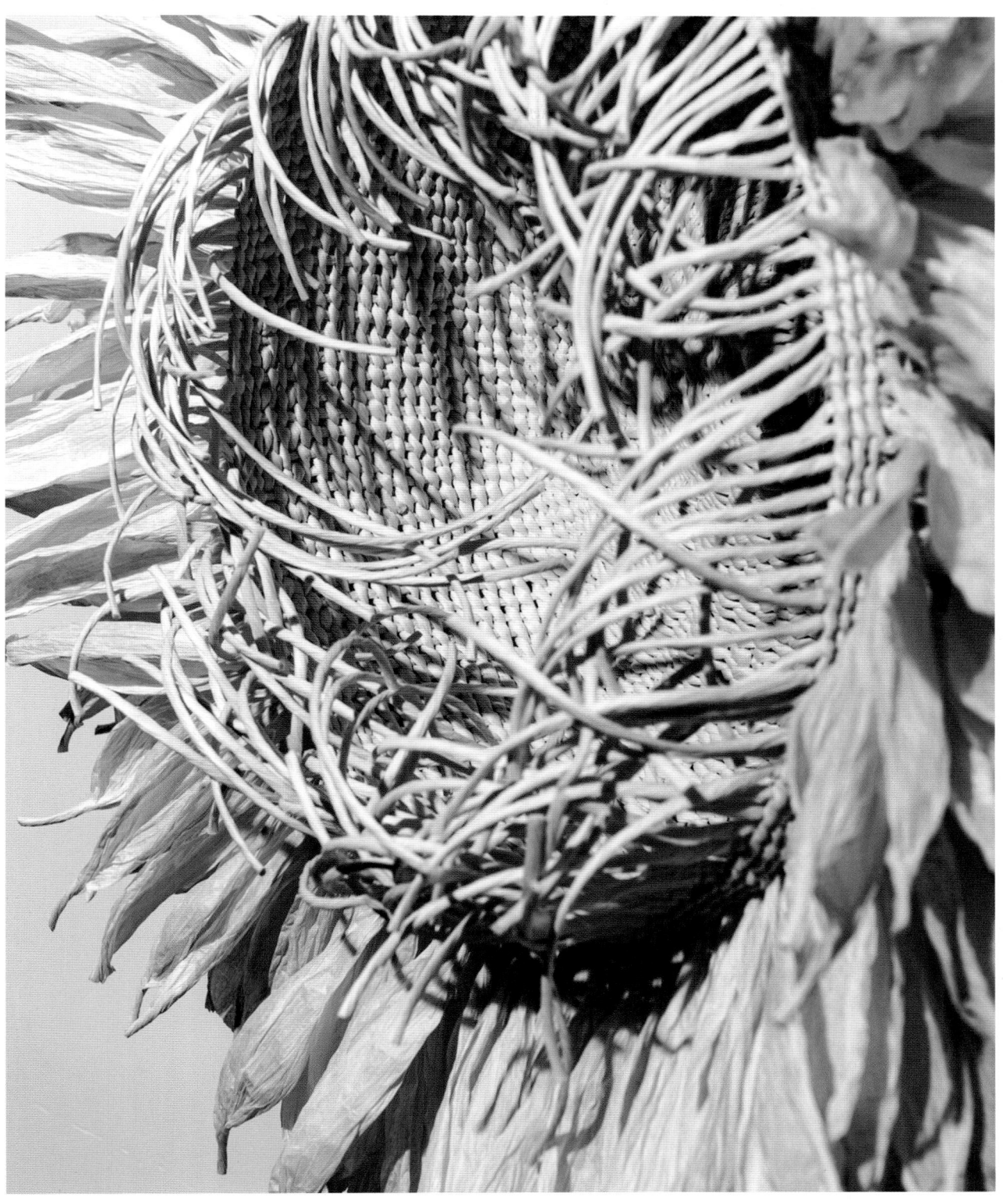

Lissa-Jane de Sailles. *Pink Bloom*, 2021. 33.5" × 33.5" × 7.5". Hand-twisted paper. *Photo courtesy of Greg Piper.* www.lissadesailles.com

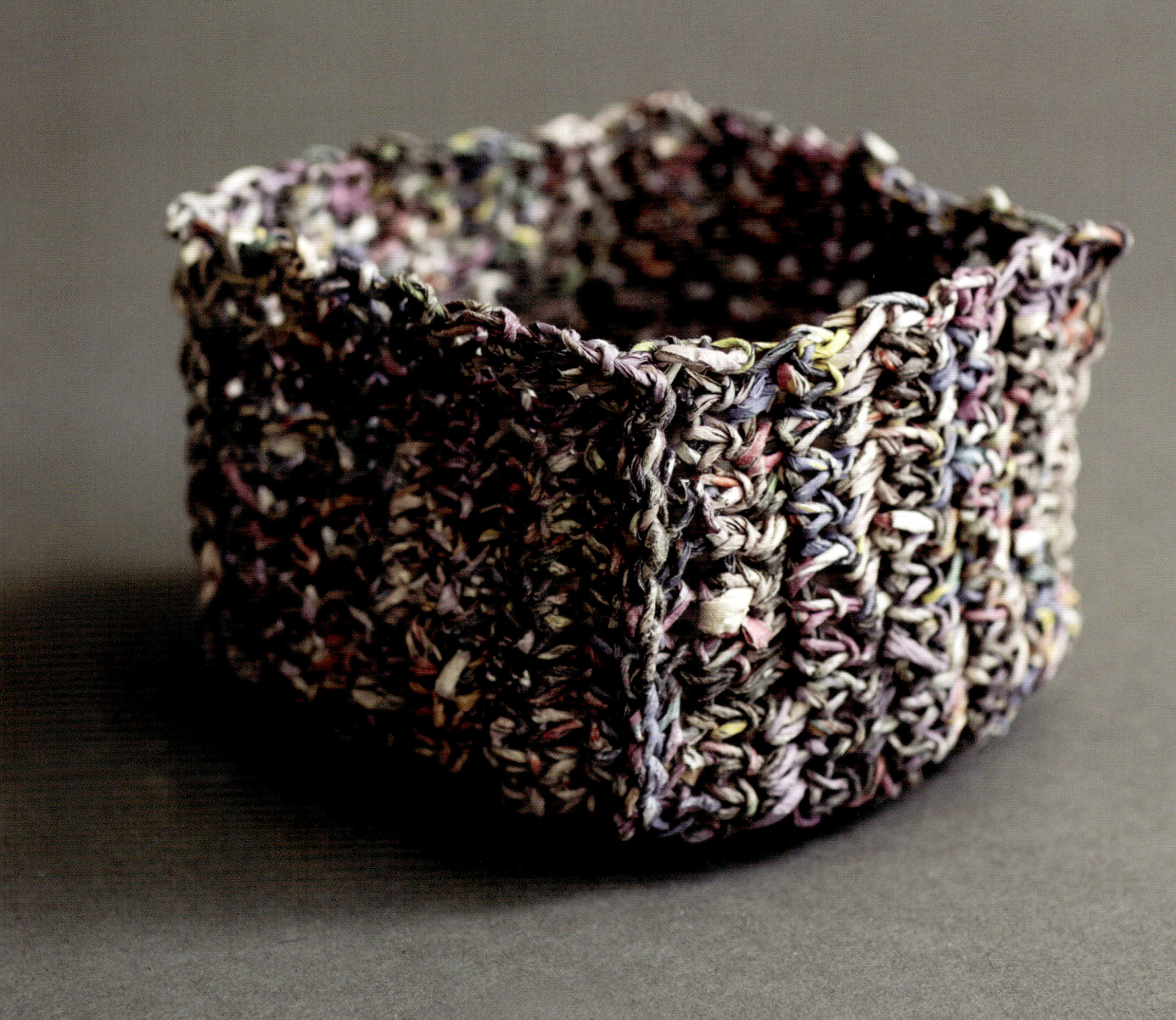

Crocheted Square Basket
by Ulrike Hagel. *Photo
courtesy of Nate Castner.*

Crocheted Square Basket

BY ULRIKE HAGEL | PAPERULI.ETSY.COM

Skill Level: Experienced

SUPPLIES

- newspaper yarn or other paper yarn, approx. 60 yards
- 1 3-mm crochet hook
- 1 large-eye blunt darning needle

INSTRUCTIONS

The project starts with crocheting the four sides of the basket in one piece. The base is then crocheted directly onto this piece.

SIDE 1

1. Chain 13.

2. Row 1: Work 1 single crochet in the second chain from the hook and each following chain. You should have 12 single crochets. Turn.

3. Rows 2–12: Chain 1. (This does not count as a stitch here and throughout; it is included to set up the next row.) Work 1 single crochet in each stitch (12 single crochets). Turn.

4. Row 13: Chain 1. Back-post single crochet 12 times. (This creates a rib effect, accentuating and stabilizing the edge of the basket.)

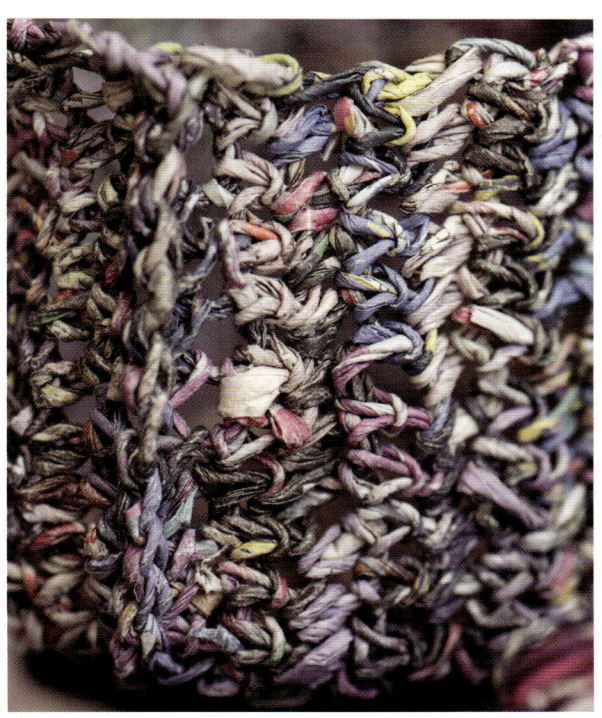

Step 4: Close-up of basket edge. *Photo courtesy of Nate Castner.*

SIDES 2 AND 3

1. Row 1: Chain 1, back-post single crochet 12 times.

2. Rows 2–12: Chain 1. Work 1 single crochet in each stitch (12 single crochets).

3. Row 13: Chain 1, back-post single crochet 12 times.

SIDE 4

1. Row 1: Chain 1, back-post single crochet 12 times.

2. Rows 2–11: Chain 1. Work 1 single crochet in each stitch (11 single crochets).

3. Row 12: Close the basket in the same way you worked the ribs between the sides: Chain 1, then work 1 back-post single crochet by inserting the hook from the back to the front into the first chain stitch of Side 1 and then from front to back in the first stitch of Side 4.

4. Repeat until the side is closed. You should have 11 back-post single crochets. Work 1 single crochet in the last stitch. You should have 12 single crochets.

BASE

The base is crocheted directly onto the edge of the fourth side.

1. Row 1: Chain 1. Work 1 single crochet in each row of the next edge. You should have 12 single crochets. Turn.

2. Rows 2–12: Chain 1. Work 1 single crochet in each stitch in the previous row. You should have 12 single crochets. Turn.

3. Secure yarn end and cut it, leaving enough yarn (~48 inches long) to sew the three open sides of the base to the sides of the baskets. (If the yarn end is too short, just add a new length of yarn.)

4. Weave in the yarn ends. The finished basket measures approximately 3.5 inches × 3.5 inches × 3.5 inches.

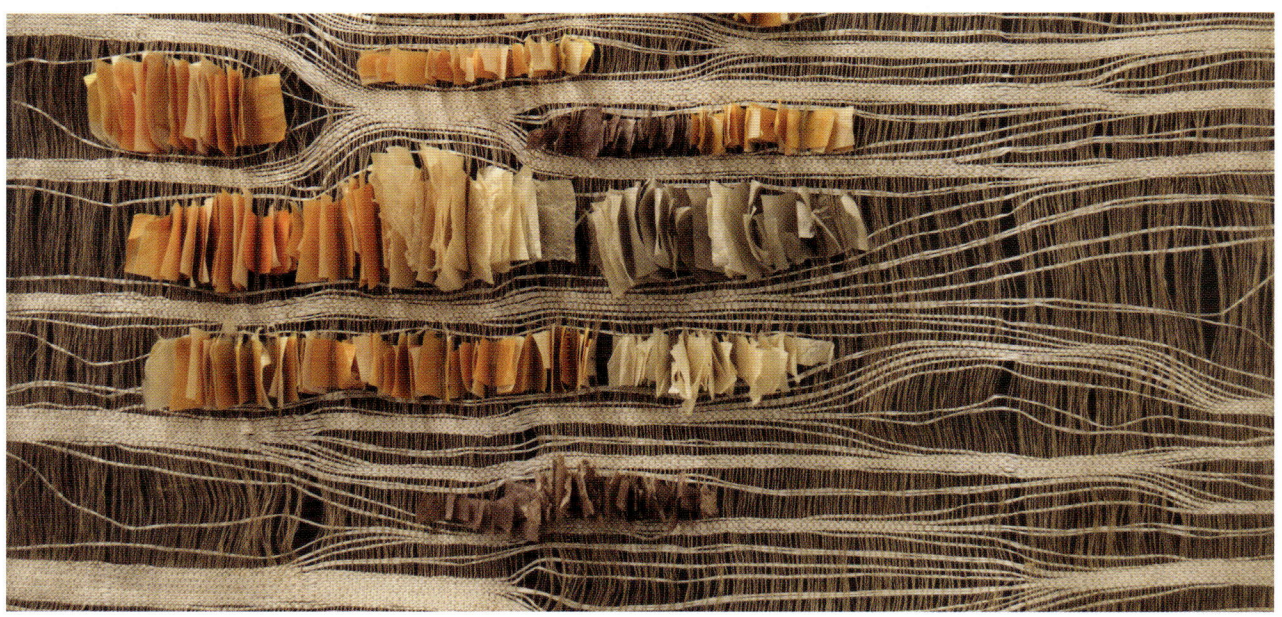

Suzi Ballenger. *At the Back of Sunset*, 2017. 15" × 27". Pine paper, fine linen, pressure-printed handmade kozo paper. Handwoven. *Photo courtesy of Suzi Ballenger. www.realfibers.com*

GLOSSARY

asa-jifu: hemp fiber bast fiber obtained from the inner bark of plants, located between the outer bark and the inner woody core

beating: separating and macerating fibers into pulp for sheet formation

cooking: boiling the raw fibers to promote separation, achieved by heating in an alkaline solution

couching: transferring a freshly made sheet of paper from a mold onto a sheet of Pellon stabilizer, papermaker's felt, or glass

Edo period: 1603 to 1868

Formica: a brand name of the original plastic laminate material used to make countertops

gampi: a bast fiber from plants in the genus *Wikstroemia*, used for Japanese handmade paper

Hollander beater: the first mechanized papermaking machine

Kamakura period: 1185 to 1333

kami: Japanese word for *paper*; also means *divinity* or *gods*

kami-ito: Japanese paper yarn or thread

kamiko: paper cloth made originally for Buddhist monks to wear during special religious ceremonies

kaminagato: a paper substitute for wood and metal

kinu-jifu: silk fiber

konjac (or konyaku): a gelatin-like substance applied to paper yarn to make it stronger and waterproof

kozo: Japan's most widely used bast fiber, from the paper mulberry tree (*Broussonetia papyrifera*); also grown in Thailand and known as *unryu* kozo

Meiji period: 1868 to 1912

men-jifu: cotton fiber

mitsumata: fiber from the shrub *Edgeworthia chrysantha*, a source for Japanese papermaking

mizuhiki: decorative knots made of stiffened and twisted paper cord or yarn; used for gift wrappings, ceremonial offerings, and accessories

mold: a rectangular wooden frame covered with a sieve-like, woven-wire surface; used for making sheets of paper

momigami: crumpled then flattened waterproof handmade paper with a bumpy surface

moro-jifu: *shifu* woven with paper warp and weft

methylcellulose glue: a non-toxic, odorless, and pH-neutral adhesive

Muromachi period: 1333 to 1573

nagashizuki: the process of forming paper sheets

neri: a viscous substance used in Japanese papermaking, usually derived from the roots of the *tororo-aoi* plant, a member of the hibiscus family

noshi: a type of ceremonial origami that serves to express good wishes, traditionally consisting of folded white paper attached to a gift containing a strip of dried abalone; considered a token of good luck

Pellon Heavyweight Interfacing: a smooth, non-woven material, often resembling paper, which does not stretch when pulled; used to couch freshly made paper sheets

pulp: the mixture of ground-up fibers and water from which paper is made

shifu: Japanese woven paper cloth

shoji: a translucent screen consisting of a wooden frame covered in paper, used as a sliding door or partition

soda ash: an alkaline substance added to water when cooking plant fibers to ready them for pulp formation

sugeta: Japanese papermaking mold comprised of the *su* (or screen) and *geta* (or hinged wooden frame)

Ts'ai Lun: an official in China's imperial court; said to have invented a forerunner of paper, although his contribution to papermaking may have been his use of maceration to break down fibers

washi: Japanese handmade paper

yomiuri: newspapers printed daily in Japan

NOTES

1. Ferris Jabr, "The Long, Knotty, World-Spanning Story of String." *Hakai Magazine*, March 6 (2018): 2

2. McArthur, Meher, and Hollis Goodall. *Washi Transformed: New Expressions in Japanese Paper*. New York: Scala Arts, 2021.

3. "SMART 2020: Enabling the Low Carbon Economy in the Information Age." 2008. http://www.smart2020.org/_assets/files/02_Smart2020Report.pdf.

4. Vito, Christopher A. "Fox School Researchers: Consumers More Likely to Recall Printed Ads Than Digital Ones." April 3, 2017. https://www.fox.temple.edu/news/2017/04/fox-school-researchers-consumers-more-likely-recall-printed-ads-digital-ones).

5. Hunter, Dard. *A Papermaking Pilgrimage to Japan, Korea and China* (New York: Pynson Printers, 1936, n.p.)

6. On UNESCO Intangible Cultural Heritage Lists, see www.ich.unesco.org.

7. Mina Takahashi, "Letter from the Editor." *Hand Papermaking Magazine*, 22 (2007): 2

8. Moriki Kayoko, "Japanese Papers: A Return to Pre-IR Washi." *Hand Papermaking Magazine*, 22 (2007): 24.

BIBLIOGRAPHY

Barrett, Timothy. *Japanese Paper-Making: Tradition, Tools and Techniques*. Warren, CT: Floating World Editions, 2006.

Hiebert, Helen. *The Papermaker's Companion*. North Adams: Storey, 2000.

Hunter, Dard. *Papermaking: The History and Technique of an Ancient Craft*. Mineola: Dover, 2011.

Jabr, Ferris. "The Long, Knotty, World-Spanning Story of String." *Hakai Magazine*, March 2018, p. 2.

Karuno, Hiroko. *Kigami and Kami-ito: Japanese Handmade Paper and Paper Thread*. Kyoto: Shikosha Publishing, 2013.

McArthur, Meher, and Hollis Goodall. *Washi Transformed: New Expressions in Japanese Paper*. New York: Scala Arts, 2021.

Takahashi, Mina. "Letter from the Editor." *Hand Papermaking Magazine*, 22 (2007): 2.

ABOUT THE AUTHOR

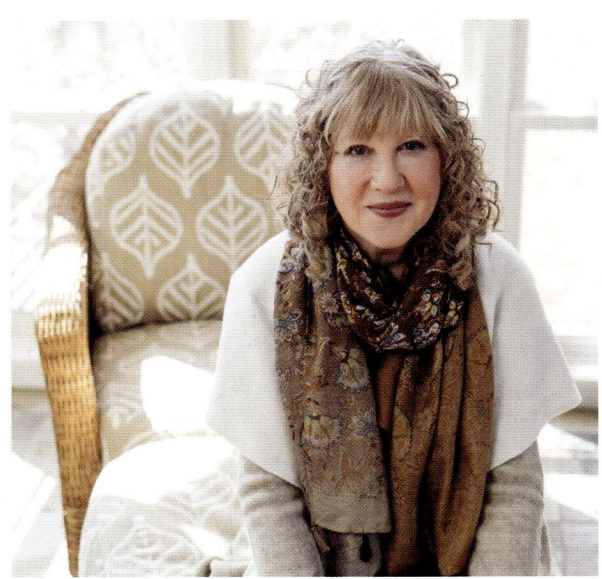

Photo: BeBoulderPhotography

Andra F. Stanton enjoys writing about and creating with fibers and fabrics in Boulder, Colorado. She first investigated fiber art for her book *Zapotec Weavers of Teotitlan*. She has gone on to explore other art forms and the people and communities who create them, including mediums like art quilting, surface design, and 3-D composition. Her previous books include *Dimensional Cloth: Sculpture by Contemporary Textile Artists*; *How Art Heals: Exploring Your Deep Feelings Using Collage*; and *Pilates for Fragile Backs*. Her work can be seen in art galleries throughout the United States.